NORTH CAROLINA
HOME BOOK

A COMPREHENSIVE HANDS-ON SOURCEBOOK TO BUILDING, REMODELING, DECORATING, FURNISHING AND LANDSCAPING A LUXURY HOME IN NORTH CAROLINA INCLUDING CHARLOTTE, RALEIGH-DURHAM AND GREENSBORO

Photo courtesy of **North Design**

PUBLISHED BY

THE
ASHLEY
GROUP

Chicago New York Los Angeles

Las Vegas Philadelphia Atlanta Detroit

Arizona South Florida Washington D.C. Colorado

San Francisco North Carolina Dallas/Fort Worth

San Diego Houston Boston Seattle Kansas City

Orange County Ohio Connecticut/Westchester County

Published By
The Ashley Group
8420 University Executive
Suite 810
Charlotte, NC 28262
704-549-3687 Fax 704-549-3695

Cahners Business Information
A Division of Reed Elsevier Inc

ISBN 1-58862-048-4

North Carolina HOME BOOK

Publisher *Thomas H. Beal*
Editor-in-Chief *Dana Felmly*
Managing Editor *Laurence P. Maloney*
Senior Editor *James Scalzitti*
Assistant Editor *Alison M. Ishihara*
Writer *Carol White*
Office Manager *Michelle Glugla*
Account Executives *Janie Hogan, Laura Kaculis, Michelle Roberts*
Group Production Director *Susan Lokaj*
Production Directors *Paul Ojeda, Catherine Wajer*
Production Manager *Kristen Axelson*
New Business Manager *Margaret S. Guzek*
Creative Director *Bill Weaver*
Senior Graphic Designer *LN Vaillancourt*
Graphic Designer *W. Keel*
Ad Service Coordinator *Sean Kealey*
Prepress *Cahners Prepress*
Printed in China by *Everbest Printing Co. Ltd*

THE ASHLEY GROUP

Group Publisher *Paul A. Casper*
Director of Publications *N. David Shiba*
Regional Director *J.D. Webster*
Group Controller *Patricia Lavigne*
Group Administration *Nicole Port, Kimberly Spizzirri*

CAHNERS BUSINESS INFORMATION

President, Global Construction and Retail Division *David Israel*
Chief Financial Officer *John Poulin*
Executive Vice President *Ronald C. Andriani*
Vice President, Finance *David Lench*

Front Cover *Planworx Architects P. A.*
Back Cover *Leo Dowell Interior Design, Photo by Joseph Laperya Photography*

Note

The premier edition of **The North Carolina Home Book** was created like most other successful products and brands are - out of need. **The Home Book** concept was originally conceived by Paul Casper, currently Group Publisher of The Ashley Group. Paul, a resident of Chicago's North Shore, at one time was planning the renovation of his home. However, he quickly discovered problems locating credible professionals to help his dream become a reality. Well, Paul's dream did become a reality - it just happens to be a different dream now! Instead of Paul simply finishing his new home, he saw the need by consumers nationwide to have a complete home resource guide at their disposal. Thus, he created the distinct **Home Book** to fulfill consumers' needs for reliable and accessible home improvement information.

After three successful years, the **Home Book** drew the attention of Cahners Business Information. In April 1999, Cahners purchased it, and since then, the **Home Book** network has grown rapidly. By the end of 2001 there were **Home Books** in 14 markets nationwide. In addition to North Carolina and Chicago, **Home Books** are available in Washington D.C., Detroit, Colorado, South Florida, Dallas/Fort Worth, Los Angeles, Atlanta, San Diego, Philadelphia, Arizona and Las Vegas. Within the next year, Home Books will be published in Houston, Seattle, Boston and Kansas City, among other cities.

Public demand for quality home improvement services continues to increase. The Ashley Group recognizes this trend, which is why we exact the same amount of dedication and hard work from ourselves that we expect from our **Home Book** advertisers. We hope our hard work rewards you with the quality craftsmanship you deserve, turning your dream house into a reality.

Congratulations on purchasing a **Home Book**. Now reward yourself by kicking back and delving through its pages. We hope you enjoy the inspiring ideas within.

Dana Felmly *Editor-in-Chief*

James Scalzitti *Senior Editor*

Why You Should Use This Book

Why You'll Want to Use the North Carolina Home Book

At times, in this high-speed information-driven culture, we can easily become lost and disoriented. Where we find information, how we find it, and how credible this information is, has become critical to consumers everywhere.

The *North Carolina Home Book* recognizes and addresses these concerns, and provides ease of use and comfort to consumers looking to build, renovate or enhance their home. As a consumer, the anxiety of searching for trustworthy, experienced housing professionals can be overwhelming.

Relief is in Sight

The *North Carolina Home Book* puts an end to this stress. It offers you, the reader, a comprehensive, hands-on guide to building, remodeling, decorating, furnishing and landscaping a home in North Carolina. The book also offers readers convenience and comfort.

Convenience

The **North Carolina Home Book** compiles the area's top home service providers with easy-to-read listings by trade. It also dissuades readers' fears of unreliable service providers by featuring many of the finest professionals available, specialists who rank among the top 10 of their respective fields in North Carolina. Their outstanding work has netted them many awards in their fields. The other listings are recommendations made by these advertisers.

The goal of the **North Carolina Home Book** creators is to provide a high quality product that goes well beyond the scope of mere Yellow Pages. Its focus is to provide consumers with credible, reliable, and experienced professionals, accompanied by photographic examples of their work.

This crucial resource was unavailable to the founders of the **North Carolina Home Book** when they were working on their own home improvement projects. This lack of information spurred them on to create the book, and to assist other consumers in finding the proper professionals that suit their specific needs. Now, thanks to the team's entrepreneurial spirit, you have the **North Carolina Home Book** at your fingertips, to guide you on your home enhancement journey.

Comfort

Embrace this book, enjoy it and relish it, because at one time it didn't exist; but now, someone has done your homework for you. Instead of running all over town, you'll find in these pages:

* More than 700 listings of professionals, specializing in 40 different trades.

      * Instructional information for choosing and working with architects, contractors, landscapers and interior designers.

      * More than 1,000 photos inspiring innovative interior and exterior modeling ideas.

      * A compilation of the area's top home enhancement service providers with easy-to-read listings by trade.

      Excitement…The North Carolina Home Book can turn your dream into a reality!

Thomas N. Be

North Carolina Home Book

About the Front Cover:
Tradition and grandeur are embodied
in this home by Planworx Architects. P. A.

Contents

Continued

219

451

157

112

31

109

North Carolina Home Book

About the Back Cover:
Elegance and comfort are combined
in this room by Leo Dowell Interiors.
Photo by Joseph Lapeyra

Contents

131

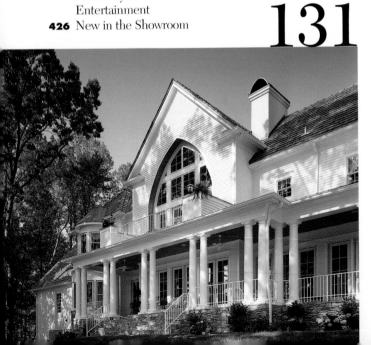

How To Use

TABLE OF CONTENTS

Start here for an at-a-glance guide to the 11 tabbed categories and numerous subcategories. The book is organized for quick, easy access to the information you want, when you want it. The Table of Contents provides an introduction to the comprehensive selection of information.

DESIGN UPDATE

Read what top home industry professionals think are the most exciting new styles, future trends and best ideas in their fields as we continue into the millennium. See even more inspiring photos of some of North Carolina's most beautiful, up-to-date luxury homes and landscapes. It's a visual feast, full of great ideas.

TIMELINES

An innovative reference tool, TimeLines gives you an at-a-glance chance to see the step-by-step progression of a home project. The projects include the building of a custom home, the remodeling of a luxury home kitchen and bath, a multi-phase landscaping project, and the interior design of several rooms. The TimeLines appear as eight-page gatefolds with glossy pictures, clearly laid-out timelines and easy-to-read paragraphs.

"HOW-TO" ARTICLES

Each tabbed section begins with a locally researched article on how to achieve the best possible result in your home building, remodeling, decorating or landscape project. These pages help take the fear and trepidation out of the process. You'll receive the kind of information you need to communicate effectively with professionals and to be prepared for the nature of the process. Each article is a step-by-step guide, aiding you in finding the materials you need in the order you'll need them.

INTERIOR DESIGN SPOTLIGHT

dedicated to showcasing the elegance and vitality of some of the most beautiful residences in the area.

This Book

DIVIDER TABS

Use the sturdy tabs to go directly to the section of the book you're interested in. A table of contents for each section's subcategories is printed on the front of each tab. Quick, easy, convenient.

LISTINGS

Culled from current, comprehensive data and qualified through careful local research, the listings are a valuable resource as you assemble the team of experts and top quality suppliers for your home project. We have included references to their ad pages throughout the book.

FEATURES!

From Interior Design Spotlight to New in the Showroom, we've devoted attention to specific areas within the various sections. We've also gone in-depth, with feature articles in the Architects and Home Builders sections.

COST ESTIMATES

If you're wondering what costs you may incur while undertaking a home project, check out our sample cost estimates. From architecture to arts and antiques, we describe a project in each chapter and give a sample cost break down for each.

BEAUTIFUL VISUALS

The most beautiful, inspiring and comprehensive collections of homes and materials of distinction in North Carolina. On these pages, our advertisers present exceptional examples of their finest work. Use these visuals for ideas as well as resources.

INDEXES

This extensive cross reference system allows easy access to the information on the pages of the book. You can check by alphabetical order or individual profession.

The A Grou

shley p

RESOURCE COLLECTION

home resource images, and strives to provide the highest
resources available to upscale consumers and professionals.
Group, visit our website at www.theashleygroup.com.
a member of the Reed Elsevier plc group, is a leading
vertical markets, including entertainment,
encompasses more than 140 Web sites as well as *Variety*,
market-leading business-to-business magazines

Design

What are the hot ideas and attitudes that are shaping homes,
Read Design Update, where top local professionals tell

Photo by **Tim Buchman**

Update

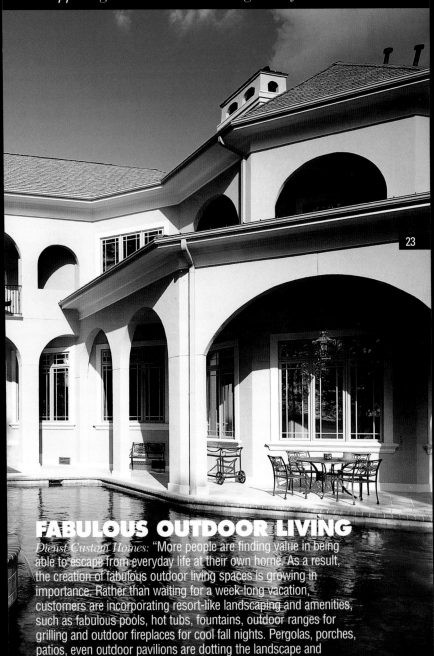

23

FABULOUS OUTDOOR LIVING

Dienst Custom Homes: "More people are finding value in being able to escape from everyday life at their own home. As a result, the creation of fabulous outdoor living spaces is growing in importance. Rather than waiting for a week-long vacation, customers are incorporating resort-like landscaping and amenities, such as fabulous pools, hot tubs, fountains, outdoor ranges for grilling and outdoor fireplaces for cool fall nights. Pergolas, porches, patios, even outdoor pavilions are dotting the landscape and transforming the traditional backyard into something truly worth coming home to."

Photo by Jim Green

DESIGN DIVERSITY

The Kitchen Specialist, Inc.: "The trend today is toward a more personal style, from European minimalism to ornate and traditional. We are seeing a desire to incorporate touches of high tech in an Old World setting, or alternatively, adding a treasured antique into a smooth, sleek design. In today's market 'anything goes.' We are comfortably combining diverse materials in the various zones of the kitchen, creating visual interest while providing maximum function."

Photo by **Bern Allen**

WATER, WATER EVERYWHERE

Garden World, Inc.: "Water features are becoming increasingly popular. Whether a formal reflecting pool or a large pond with waterfalls, this item becomes the focal point of the landscape. It is the most alive area in the whole garden, and may include the magnificent color of Koi or the sweet perfume of lotus or waterlilies. If proper attention goes into each detail, you will have a peaceful, private sanctuary that will provide enjoyment for years to come."

SOFTER, WARMER CONTEMPORARY

Triangle Design Kitchens, Inc.: "Today's contemporary kitchens are showing a sophisticated look with the use of exotic natural materials mixed with stainless steel and industrial finishes. Look for exotic wood veneers in both silk and high gloss finishes paired with stainless steel appliances and countertops. Design accents are added using metallic painted finishes, also available in silk or high gloss. The fronts of doors are often pillowed, rather than perfectly flat. The look is softer, warmer and much more exciting than the bare, monochromatic contemporary European look of years past."

THE TROPICAL LOOK

Blacklion:
"The ease and comfort of tropical designs and the look of rattan furniture is evident through the trends we are seeing in home décor and design. Shades of green and tans complement this comfortable yet stylish look, which can work in any area of the home. You do not have to live in a tropical climate to enjoy this new design movement. Subtle decorative accessories, such as a bamboo lamp or palm tree candlesticks, can add the feeling of the tropics to a home."

KNOWLEDGEABLE BUYERS

Carole F. Smyth Interiors: "Homebuyers these days are more knowledgeable than ever before about the building process and the materials used in their homes. Years ago, a builder did not have to worry about the type of plumbing fixtures and lighting he used, the texture of the drywall, or the brand and finish of appliances. The public looked only at the attractiveness of the facility, what rooms were provided, and if the layout was acceptable. Today's people are knowledgeable on many of the items in their homes, and they are not willing to accept mediocrity."

PUTTING AROUND

Estate Golf by Osborn:

"An increasing trend for custom homeowners with a passion for golf is incorporating a 'golf haven' into their estate or weekend home. They are seeking a refuge where they can decompress while honing their golf skills on a putting green that performs to the standards of exclusive private club greens. Yet their passion also demands a putting green design that is in harmony with and enhances the landscape, requiring minimal maintenance and providing lasting beauty."

A BREATH OF FRESH AIR

Building Graphics Architecture: "The desire for authentic detailing has reintroduced older design styles to the housing industry, along with the use of a variety of materials that has been like a breath of fresh air. You see the use of cedar shake siding and stone accents. Beadboard is used on all types of ceilings, as well as for wainscoting in many interior areas. Recycled heart pine flooring accents are used in many of these authentically detailed homes. Copper and tile are used more frequently for a roofing material, and simplified roof structures are taking the place of the cut-up complicated framer-busters of the past."

SIMPLER WINDOWS STRONGER WALLS

Reid's Decorating, Inc.: "Our clients have started to use simpler window treatments, but more elaborate trims. The use of sheer is back, in every form; plain, etched, dotted, embroidered, printed, linen, silk, striped, patterned and embellished. Chenille fabrics are still the favorite for heavy use areas, and silks for the dressy windows. Stronger wall colors are coming back, the neutrals once more giving way to color."

ROOMS SPREAD OUT

Spain Construction: "Space planning is important with today's families. We want room to spread out! Kitchens, dens, sunrooms and dining areas are open and flow into each other. Current remodeling projects enlarge the small, closed-in areas of the 1950s and 1960s and now offer views to other rooms and the outdoors. Accents on cabinetry, millwork and lighting create a sense of warmth and community for family enjoyment."

27

THE NEW HOME THEATER

Advanced Visual Environments: "The concept of the home theater has evolved to describe more than the standard vision of a large format screen within a themed room. Home theater systems now encompass not only audio/video and film, but also live broadcast events, HDTV, Internet media and video gaming, all at the same time."

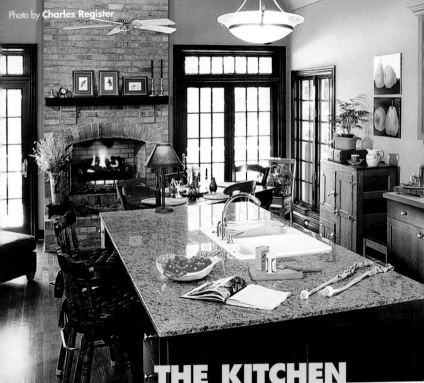

THE KITCHEN RETURNS HOME

RETURN TO THE STONE AGE

Architectural Concept Stone: "**Architectural precast stone is a way many homeowners are achieving the look of real stone without the high cost. Custom precast designs can be used for decks, columns, balustrades, railings, fireplaces, exterior trim elements, planters, urns, fountains, and pool and spa copings. The product is designed to last a lifetime just like the natural stone it imitates.**"

Shaw/Davis Architects, P.A.: "Although kitchens have always been a focal point of activity, they are often not designed to become a home within a home. Too much emphasis has been placed on its functionality rather than its livability. We are seeing a trend toward enlarging the kitchen area slightly and adding such things as a fireplace, comfortable chairs, and a small breakfast table, to bring a sense of home back into the kitchen."

INFORMAL LIVING

Pfahl Custom Builders, Inc.: "Homeowners today want less formal space and more informal living areas. They are requesting large family rooms which open onto the outdoor living areas and flow nicely into the kitchen and eating areas."

CURB APPEAL

Swimmer Construction: "There is a renewed emphasis on increasing a home's 'curb appeal.' Clients want their homes to express who they are, both in the interior spaces and on the exterior facade. Solutions range from simple add-ons, to more complex structural alterations. No matter what the size, today's homes require extended landings, roofing additions and innovative lighting."

CLASSICAL CHARM

De Santana Stone Company, Inc.: "Homeowners are finding new and unique uses for handcarved stone. Some of these uses include Corinthian column table bases, which add a classic look to the dining area, and full columns, in any style, which create exciting structural textures that blend beautifully with the new generation of architectural styles. The Old World charm of natural stone can also be applied to balustrades, planters, facings and fountains."

DECORATIVE GLASS HOUSES

Stained Glass Overlay of Charlotte, Inc.: "Our clients have been incorporating decorative glass in a varied array of settings, from sidelights to shower stalls, and kitchen cabinets to mirrors. They are working their own custom designs, along with hundreds of colors and textures, to form glorious windows and doors."

WOODS WITH CHARACTER

Carolina Kitchen Studios: "In contrast to cold, minimalist designs, many homeowners are turning to heavily distressed woods that have a warm, 'lived-in' look. Instead of eliminating the mineral streaks, wormholes, burl grain, tight knots or other tree growth irregularities inherent in woods like cherry, these characteristics are augmented with hand-distressing, for a unique, antique-textured quality. Glazes further accent the profiles and distress marks."

35

FAMILY-FRIENDLY

Audio Video One: "Homeowners are focusing more on their families these days, and that means spending more quality time at home. They're enhancing the home theater experience with automated controls, in addition to ensuring that their other electronic components can be controlled simply and comfortably."

RUGS UNDERFOOT

Rug Crafters, Inc.: "In the new millennium, we are finding there is increased interest in decorating with rugs. The trend in design is leaning toward a less cluttered look with simpler lines, yet still extremely personalized and functional. By creatively combining colors, design elements and sizes, a unique rug, reflecting the client's creativity and desires, can be fashioned. With rugs, the possibilities are endless."

FUN & GAMES

Nostalgic Sports and Games: "As baby boomers age up and have more available discretionary income, they are creating 'play rooms' complete with upscale furniture, pool tables, custom bars, poker/game tables, and unique wall décor and accessories. Many couples also want the 'nostalgic' look in their game room and are looking for a jukebox, foosball tables, classic pinball machines and arcade-style video games. Media rooms are not complete without classic theater-style popcorn machines, soda fountains and movie artwork. However, it's not just for the adults. Parents are creating home entertainment environments where their children want to stay home and entertain their friends."

INTRICATE STONEWORK

M.R. Marble & Tile: "Intricate patterns and detailed work using natural stones and natural-looking tile is quickly becoming the most popular way for people to turn their living space into a unique and beautiful home."

SIMPLE BALANCE

Gaye Mitchum Interiors: "People are seeking simplicity and balance in their lives and homes. They are now looking for spaces that will nurture their spirits and comfort their souls."

CONTROLLING TECHNOLOGY

Smart Home Innovations: "Technology throughout the home is becoming easier to use and control. Systems for music, home theaters, security, lighting and climate control are evolving to the point where they will all be controlled from one network, or a device as small as a PDA. Homeowners will also be able to routinely check on their homes from afar via the Internet."

Photo by **Robert Bailey**

38

ARTISAN-
INSPIRED WALLS

Celtic Wall by Belgard: "Homeowners have been moving away from single row brick work in their retaining walls, in favor of a more artisan-inspired construction, with alternating forms and open layouts. They want texture and angles, things that add a third dimension to their walls. Just like the vertical aspects it enhances, the retaining wall comes alive by incorporating the roughness and irregularity of natural stone. The choice of colors and shapes is vast, and today's retaining walls lend themselves to any type of surroundings."

40

RUSTIC STONE

Laufen Tile & Stone: "Natural and rustic are the two words that best sum up the sought-after designs in tile and stone today. Advances in ceramic tile manufacturing techniques mean that tiles can naturally replicate the look of natural stone, but are still easy to maintain. Slates, limestones, marbles and travertines are popular in antiqued looks, tumbled surfaces and chiseled edges. Additionally, the classic polished granite countertop is gaining popularity, as product costs decrease."

MARRYING FUNCTION
WITH BEAUTY

DCI Kitchen & Bath: "The hallmark of great kitchen design and engineering is a combination of beauty with function, to best meet the needs of today's families. Our clients like designs with discrete functional work zones, which allow essential appliances to be showcased for design drama. The microwave may be nestled behind a retractable, flip-up cabinet door, while refrigeration is integrated into a tall armoire. This marriage of form, function and beauty provides a winning combination."

42

FOCUS ON DESIGN

TG&R Landscape Group: "Architectural elements in the garden, such as a fountain symmetrically located behind an entry gate or seat walls around a lowered patio, create a focus for the eye to draw visitors in. Combining a mixture of landscape materials, elements and textures makes small spaces seem larger, transforming them into private, welcoming retreats."

44

THE HEARTH OF A HOME

Bonnie Fleming, LLC: "Homeowners don't want their kitchens to look like kitchens anymore. They want them to look more like the rest of the home. We're seeing refrigerators and dishwasher designs that look like cabinet drawers, and ovens without dials, buttons, clocks or electronic gadgetry. Ovens with the look of old-fashioned wood stoves, yet offering today's modern convenience, are very popular."

COMFORTABLE & SENSIBLE

Wolfe Homes: "Custom home clients are preparing for the second half of their lives, filled with visits from parents, college students, adult children and grandkids. Clients are specifying a first-floor guest suite incorporating a private bath. First-floor master suites are more spacious, complete with an adjacent sitting area. Master baths no longer sprawl, but are more elegant featuring built-in cabinetry with the look of fine furniture. Living rooms are disappearing, while media rooms and digitally wired offices are popular. Cozy hearth rooms are being added just off the kitchen, and family room cathedral ceilings are being traded for the utility of second-floor space."

THE NECESSITY OF SPACE

West Fourth Landscape Architecture: "Life continues to be too busy for modern lives. Vacations don't come frequently enough to help us deal with the mounting day-to-day stress. As a result, more people are discovering the necessity and pleasure that a well-planned outdoor space provides. Opening the interior of one's home and expanding the indoor-outdoor relationships to the site greatly increases the living area. Water features, special lighting, local or exotic building materials and plantings all combine to produce the feeling of friendly spaces that are always available."

EDUCATE THYSELF

Carolina Audio Consultants: "**Customer involvement is the key to the ultimate enjoyment of state-of-the-art audio-video and home theater systems. It's important to become educated about the many options available and actively involved in the design process. Working as a team with the audio-video designer gives clients the knowledge to create a system that meets and exceeds their expectations and requirements.**"

Photo by **Jenny Weiler**

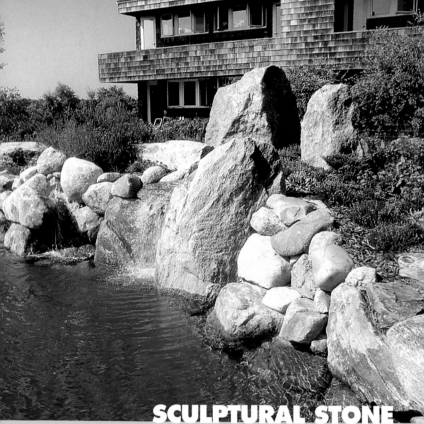

SCULPTURAL STONE

Peter Bochenek & Associates: "Homeowners today want more than a garden that is 'just another pretty face.' They want front yards to welcome them home, and back yards to take them away from the stress of everyday life. The ingredients that create a sense of timeless magic are the sound of falling water, an envelope of green texture, and ancient stone with a rich, weathered patina. When correct in scale and properly set, stone becomes a sculptural element for the landscape that provides a powerful and calming influence. The design elements merge into the landscape, allowing the boundary between old and new to vanish."

COVERED WITH STONE

Wagstaff Tile: "Natural stone and tile are becoming integral parts of many areas of the home. Many homeowners are covering entire floors with beautiful travertines and limestones. Tile sizes are getting larger, with 18" by 18" and 16" by 24" formats. Contemporary floor plans now flow between foyer, family rooms, dining rooms and kitchens. The timeless look of natural stone, as well as the excellent stone lookalikes being produced today, complete the feeling for those homeowners who want Old World ambiance and a Mediterranean open floor plan."

A VARIETY OF USES

Marble and Granitech, Inc.: " Many homeowners in this area have used natural marble in different ways to add a touch of elegance to their homes. Everything from marble window sills, shower floors, countertops, foyers and walkway stones to the entire exterior of a building are just a few of the applications possible with this beautiful and luxurious building material."

ARTISTIC LICENSE

Ed Council: "Decorative wall painting has been with us from cave-dwelling times to the present. We are happy to see this tradition continuing in today's finer homes. Present-day artists offer a wide range of subject matter from which to choose; from faux painting to trompe l'oeil to complex custom murals-traditional to contemporary, classical to whimsical. These paintings can be done directly on the walls in your home, to open up a room or depict a subject interesting to the homeowner. The options are limitless."

CLASSIC
INNOVATIVE STYLE

Impel, Inc.: "Home design elements from central Europe – Germany, Austria, Czechoslovakia, northern France and Italy - are very popular today. True casement windows, balconies, window boxes, wrought-iron detailing and exterior gaslights, along with rich, luxurious faux finishes, capture the character of these European homes. At the same time, the latest innovative materials that combine richness of detail with durability and ease of maintenance are being employed for flexibility in design and cost-effective construction."

IMPORTANT TRANSITIONS

Dina Lowery's Studio of Design: "Designers and homeowners alike realize that every space is important: staircases, hallways and corridors transition us from one space to another in the home. Compositions of artwork and accessories are vital in carrying a mood from one space to another."

RETREAT INTO LANDSCAPING

Island Design L.L.C.: "The expression of art, atmosphere and functional value should always be the priority in landscape design. With today's hectic lifestyles, homeowners should consider their landscape to be a retreat for escape and solitude."

IMAGINATIVE DESIGN

Hardscapes: "Today, more than ever, homeowners know the importance of stellar design and impeccable workmanship when it comes to enhancing the beauty and value of their property. Quality brick paver driveways, patios, and parking areas, along with well-thought-out and executed landscape walls and retaining wall systems add the finishing touch."

ACCENTS ON HARDWOOD

Allied Flooring Products: "Hardwood flooring is no longer just a straight expanse of wood. Custom borders and accents add interest, style and individuality. Borders can be as simple or ornate as your imagination will allow. Selected custom accents, using a variety of hardwood species, give a room added dimension and warmth. Others create a more formal look and help complete a room with a stylish finishing touch."

INTEGRATED TECHNOLOGY

Innovative Systems: "The keyword in home entertainment today is integration. With significant technological advances in home theater, high definition television, plasma screens, audio and video distribution, lighting control, computer networking and internet-based control systems; our ability to integrate each of these complex systems into a seamless, easy-to-use home entertainment system is critical. At the same time, homeowners want the components of these systems to be as invisible as possible, to minimize the impact on the home's décor."

52

Photo by **Stanley Capps**

Photo by **John Martinelli**

CEILINGS ARE WHAT'S UP

Miller Architecture: "Ceilings offer an under-developed canvas, and it is becoming easier to decorate overhead. The materials do not have to be as durable as other surfaces, so high levels of detail, texture, color or matte finishes of natural woods are possible. There are more places to find wood pulp and plaster medallions, with the proliferation of companies supplying these products making a comeback. With access to the Internet, stock components and skilled tradesmen are closer to the consumer than ever before."

SERIOUS SPORTS

Heavenly Backyards by Sport Court: "Sports enthusiasts are demanding more from their backyards than ever before. Custom designed basketball and racquet courts, roller hockey fields, even putting greens are being installed in both new and existing construction. The new variety of colors, designs and surfaces not only blend with, but actually enhance the outdoor landscape."

HOMESTYLE KITCHENS

Leo Dowell Interiors, Inc.: "My favorite times growing up in Mount Airy (that's right, 'Mayberry RFD') were helping my mom prepare dishes for the family. I always felt at ease in that kitchen. Over the years, however, kitchens have become sterile, institutional places, where even the ketchup -bottle looks out of place. But homeowners want to return to those welcoming kitchens of days past. They want kitchens that say 'come on in, take off your hat and stay awhile.'"

A SHARING THE VISION

North Design: "With such trends as home theaters, computers in about every area of a home, family workout spaces and large gathering kitchens, design has become a close collaboration of the client, builder and design professional, all working as a team."

WELCOMING GUEST BATHS

Hailey Company LLC:
"Homeowners are demanding more design and style in their guest bath and powder rooms. Vanities with Old World finishes created by a careful selection of glazes and application techniques hold special appeal. Larger countertops afford room for a decorative lamp, or for visitors to place a handbag. These sophisticated furnishings with storage for towels and other necessities are essential. Homeowners take pride in knowing guests will be treated to a warm, yet functional room."

Photo by **Alexander Photographics**

❽ TEAMWORK

WHJ Design, Inc.: "As custom homes continue to become more personalized with all the options and advances in technology available, there is a major shift toward a total group approach. Designer, decorator, landscape designer and contractor all work together, providing input from the early stages, to create the most complete and personalized end product for the client."

❽

VARIETY OF STYLES

Olde World Reclamation:
" 'Variety is the spice of life,' the saying goes, and we are increasingly seeing examples of that. Our clients are interested in a variety of styles, from rustic English pine and French Country to the flowing elegance of Art Nouveau. Classic 18th century fountains are being moved indoors, to merge home and garden into one continuous space. All of these styles continue to make architectural antiques more exciting and desirable to the homeowner and gardener."

57

EUROPEAN STYLE

Planworx Architecture, P.A.: "We're seeing more homes adopting elements of European design, both in exterior and interior details. Architectural details include swooping roofs, precast moldings around windows and doors, and custom garages with columns and recessed trellises accenting the space between doors. Inside, curved stairways, decorative niches, walk-in pantries and cabinets with feet embody this European style."

WOOD-BURNING OVENS

Unique Homes of Charlotte, Inc.: "Wood-fired chicken, fish, roasted vegetables and a variety of pizzas, brochettes and breads are tantalizing taste buds everywhere. Our clients want these tastes satisfied at home as well, which accounts for the popularity of wood-burning ovens in today's custom homes. These imported, hand-built masonry ovens make a statement and become truly unique conversation pieces, while stimulating all the senses."

Photo by **Robert Baily**

Photo by E. Ward

UNIQUE HARDSCAPES

Creative Pavers: "In today's market, individuality is the key. Our clients are looking for something to separate them from their neighbor. Whether it be a paver driveway or a courtyard patio, they want to be different. Fortunately, hardscape manufacturers have responded to the demand. The development of new pavement and retaining wall styles has allowed homeowners to achieve a look all their own. The development of new materials, coupled with homeowners' willingness to create something unique, has made our business a ton of fun."

OLD WORLD STYLE

Charlotte Cabinets, Inc.: "Today's kitchens and bathrooms are being designed in a traditional, Old World style. Homeowners want the cabinetry and fixtures in their kitchens and baths to look more like fine furniture, with detailed crown moldings, turned posts, fluted columns and classic feet. They are also looking for more architectural detail. Warmer wood tones and creamy glazes are popular, along with inset doors and the Shaker look. More appliances are being paneled to 'melt' into the design, for that true custom look."

61

GLOBAL INFLUENCES

Custom Cabinetry, Inc.: "The kitchen is more than a room; it is the epicenter of the home. Its design should be tailored to the needs of the homeowner, while creating the ambiance of comfort and function. Never before have so many design options been available for the kitchen. The influences from global cultures are having a creative impact on American kitchens. A multitude of styles and textures, incorporating natural surfaces, materials and subtle lighting are creating a new elegance in the kitchen."

UNIQUE PERSONAL STATEMENTS

Treeline Landscaping & Nursery: "Even though function and practicality are important elements in the design process, landscapes are expected to inspire various feelings in homeowners. Their effect is emotional as well as practical. The home is a personal expression, and the landscape should be a personal statement as unique as the home itself."

WARM AND LIVABLE

Southern Structures, Inc.: "Although people are generally building larger homes, they still want them to feel very comfortable and livable. We are incorporating a significant number of amenities into new homes, from home theaters to indoor pools. The combination of new, sophisticated materials with vintage, rescued specialty items, are blended together to create a very warm new home."

STONE ELEGANCE

Forum: "Natural stone, with its elegant beauty and durability, is the trend of the new millennium. Limestone, marble, granite and other natural stone products are available in many different finishes and colors to give designers and architects the

CUSTOM FIREPLACES

Innovative Building Products: "While a fireplace has always been coveted by homeowners, today's innovative designs allow fireplaces to go where they have not gone before. Vent-free fireplaces can be built into an elaborate stone room divider. Even a television can be placed directly above a vent-free fireplace to create a true center focus in a family room. Where a vent-free unit is not permitted, such as most bedrooms, or where wood-burning applications are not feasible, a direct-vent fireplace is an ideal way to give a room that special glow."

QUALITY OVER QUANTITY

Meadows Custom Homes: "Our clients these days are opting for quality over quantity. With land costs increasing and the available land decreasing, the trend is toward building homes on smaller, more manicured lots. People are directing more attention to their landscapes. Inside, whole house automation systems, which allow a homeowner to control the home's operations from one central location or even outside the home, are increasing in popularity. These 'smart home' systems allow a homeowner, for example, to turn on the air conditioning from the office or from the car, on the ride home."

67

68

BEAUTIFUL INDULGENCE

KRM Design Ltd.: "Beauty is the distinctive design element of today's master bath suite, providing a comfortable and lavish space. Materials and furnishings include inlaid exotic wood floors, baroque carved millwork, marble, granite and limestone. These surfaces, along with Venetian glass and painted finishes, are often used to create a warm, intimate, and often indulgent room in which to relax and luxuriate."

THE SANCTUARY OF HOME

David Thomas & Associates, Inc.: "The home is once again becoming the sanctuary for people with hectic, busy lives. We generally have only our homes to express our individuality, be it our creative or spiritual sides. A place to unite families, we use the home also as our entertainment center, with better-equipped kitchens, more casual furnishings, home theaters, swimming pools and relaxing spas. Homes are quieter nowadays, with insulated interior walls, double-glazed, insulated windows and well designed HVAC systems."

CHARACTER & STYLE

G. Allen Scruggs, A.S.I.D.: "The aesthetic energy generated by combining old with new, rough with smooth, in textiles, accessories, even furniture and lighting gives a home character and style. For example, the addition of antique architectural elements in a new home, such as large-scale antique doors at the entrance, a reassembled antique marble chimney breast in the living room, or an iron balustrade retro-fitted for the staircase, creates a unique, interesting interior."

THE NOBILITY OF STONE

Belgard/Oldcastle: "The 'old stone' style reigns supreme in paving stones, but with a new treatment, inspired by the mythical origins of Greek cities and the heritage of the Old World. Adding an undeniably historical aspect, the 'aged' pavers adopt daring curves and twists thanks to a modular design that can be adapted to the grandest projects. Through it all, the nobility of stone endures."

WATER GARDENS

Mic & Whick's Landscaping, Inc.: "Homeowners are discovering that water gardening is not only enjoyable, but a therapeutic method of reconnecting with nature. Water gardens provide people with a splash of tranquility in their own backyards, a way to recover from the stress of a long day at work."

INTERIOR DESIGNERS

CONTRACTORS STORY

KITCHEN & BATH

DESIGN UPDATE EDITORIAL PAGES

ART & ANTIQUES

HOME FURNISHINGS

LANDSCAPERS

NEW IN THE SHOWROOM FEATURE

Just a Sampling
of the Spectacular
pages in your
Home Book

Finally...
North Carolina's Own
Home & Design
Sourcebook

The ***North Carolina Home Book*** is your final destination when searching for home remodeling, building and decorating resources. This comprehensive, hands-on sourcebook to building, remodeling, decorating, furnishing and landscaping a luxury home is required reading for the serious and discriminating homeowner. With more than 500 full-color, beautiful pages, the ***North Carolina Home Book*** is the most complete and well-organized reference to the home industry. This hard-cover volume covers all aspects of the process, includes listings of hundreds of industry professionals, and is accompanied by informative and valuable editorial discussing the most recent trends. Ordering your copy of the ***North Carolina Home Book*** now can ensure that you have the blueprints to your dream home, in your hand, today.

O R D E R F O R M

Home Books

12 Tips
For Pursuing
Quality

1. Assemble a Team of Professionals During Preliminaries.
Search out and value creativity.

2. Educate Yourself on What to Expect
But also be prepared to be flexible in the likely event of set-backs.

3. Realize the Value and Worth of Design.
It's the best value for your investment.

4. Be Involved in the Process.
It's more personally satisfying and yields the best results.

5. Bigger Isn't Better – Better is Better.
Look for what produces quality and you'll never look back.

6. Understand the Process.
Be aware of products, prices and schedules, to be a productive part of the creative team.

7. Present a Realistic Budget.
Creative, workable ideas can be explored.

8. Create the Right Environment.
Mutual respect, trust and communication get the job done.

9. There Are No Immediate Miracles.
Time is a necessary component in the quest for quality.

10. Have Faith in Yourself.
Discover your own taste and style.

11. Plan for the Future.
Lifestyles and products aren't static.

12. Do Sweat the Details.
Establish the discipline to stay organized.

NORTH CAROLINA
HOME BOOK

8420 University Executive., Ste 810, Charlotte, NC 28262 702-549-3687 fax 704-549-3695

BUILDINGRAPHICS
ARCHITECTURE

7400 CARMEL EXECUTIVE PARK
TEL. 704.542.1498
SUITE 150 • CHARLOTTE, NC 28226
FAX 704.542.1499

www.planworx.com | 919-846-8100 | 5711 Six Forks Rd., Suite 100, Raleigh, NC 27609

Planworx
Architecture

The First Step

An architect is the first step in realizing your vision for your new or remodeled home. This professional is not only skilled in the technical areas of space planning, engineering and drafting, but also happens to be an expert in materials, finishes, energy efficiency, even landscaping. An architect takes the time to find out how you live, what your needs are, and how you'd like to see your dreams come to fruition, all the while keeping your budget in mind. He or she can assemble seemingly disparate elements into a design that combines your needs with your desires, with grace, beauty and efficiency. We have the privilege of featuring the finest of these creative, technically proficient problem solvers to help you bring your ultimate home to life.

Architects

WHAT'S YOUR LIFESTYLE?

- Who lives in the house now?
- Who will live there in the future?
- Who visits and for how long?
- Do you like traditional, contemporary or eclectic design?
- Why are you moving or remodeling?
- What aspects of your current home need to be improved upon?
- Do you like functional, minimalist design, or embellishments and lots of style?
- Do you entertain formally or informally?
- How much time will you spend in the master bedroom? Is it spent reading, watching TV, working or exercising?
- What are the primary functions of the kitchen?
- Do you need a home office?
- Do you like lots of open space or little nooks and crannies?
- What kind of storage do you need?

BRINGING IDEAS TO LIFE

Whether you're building your dream home in the city, a second vacation home, or remodeling your home in the suburbs, it takes a team to design and build a high quality residential project. A team of an architect, builder, interior designer, kitchen and bath designer, and landscape architect/designer should be assembled very early in the process. When these five professionals have the opportunity to collaborate before ground is broken, you'll reap the rewards for years to come. Their blend of experience and ideas can give you insights into the fabulous possibilities of your home and site you never considered. Their association will surely save you time, money and eventually frustration.

THE ARCHITECT — MAKING THE DREAM REAL

Licensed architects provide three basic, easily defined tasks. First, they design, taking into account budget, site, owner's needs and existing house style. Second, they produce the necessary technical drawings and specifications to accomplish the desires of their clients, and explain to a contractor in adequate detail what work needs to be done. Lastly, architects participate in the construction process. This straightforward mission requires more than education.

It requires listening. The best architects have gained their status by giving their clients exactly what they want - even when those clients have difficulty articulating what that is. How? By creatively interpreting word pictures into real pictures. By eliciting the spirit of the project and following that spirit responsibly as they develop an unparalleled design.

It requires experience. Significant architects, such as those included in your Home Book, maintain a reputation for superiority because their buildings are stunningly conceived, properly designed and technically sound. If a unique, steeply pitched roof was custom-designed for you by a licensed architect with an established reputation, you can be confident that it is buildable.

Suggestions by an experienced architect can add value and interest to your new home or remodeling project. He or she may suggest you wire your home for the technology of the future, frame up an attic for future use as a second floor, or build your countertops at varying levels to accommodate people of different heights

This area is blessed with many talented architects. It's not uncommon for any number of them to be working on a luxury vacation retreat in another country or a unique second home in another state. Their vision and devotion to design set a standard of excellence for dynamic and uncompromising quality.

WORKING WITH AN ARCHITECT

The best relationships are characterized by close collaborative communication. The architect is the person you're relying on to take your ideas, elevate them to the highest level, and bring them to life in a custom design that's never been built before. So take your time in selecting the architect. It's not unusual for clients to spend two or three months interviewing prospective architects.

In preparation for the interview process, spend time fine-tuning your ideas. Put together an Idea Notebook (See the sidebar 'Compile an Idea Notebook'). Make a wish list that includes every absolute requirement and every fantasy you've ever wanted in a home. Visit builder's models to discover what 3,000 sq. ft. looks like in comparison to 6,000 sq. ft., how volume ceilings impact you or what loft living feels like. Look at established and new neighborhoods to get ideas about the relationship between landscaping and homes, and what level of landscaping you want.

GOOD COMMUNICATION SETS THE TONE

The first meeting is the time to communicate all of your desires for your new home or remodeling project, from the abstract to the concrete. You're creating something new, so be creative in imprinting your spirit and personality on the project. Be bold in expressing your ideas, even if they are not fully developed or seem unrealistic. Share your Idea Notebook and allow the architect to keep it as plans are being developed. Be prepared to talk about your lifestyle, because the architect will be trying to soak up as much information about you and your wishes as possible.

• Be frank about your budget. Although some clients are unrestricted by budgetary concerns, most must put some control on costs, and good architects expect and respect this. Great ideas can be achieved on a budget, and the architect will tell you what can be achieved for your budget.

• However, sticking to your budget requires tremendous self-discipline. If there's a luxury you really want, (a second laundry room, a built-in aquarium) it's probably just as practical to build it into your design from the outset, instead of paying for it in a change order once building has begun. ••

COMPILE AN IDEA NOTEBOOK

It's hard to put an idea into words, but so easy to show with a picture. Fill a good-sized notebook with plain white paper, tuck a roll of clear tape and a pair of scissors into the front flap, and you've got an Idea Notebook. Fill it with pictures, snapshots of homes you like, sketches of your own, little bits of paper that show a color you love, notes to yourself on your priorities and wishes. Circle the parts of the pictures and make spontaneous notes: "Love the finish on the cabinets," "Great rug," "Don't want windows this big." Show this to your architect, and other team members. Not only will it help keep ideas in the front of your mind, but will spark the creativity and increase understanding of the entire team.

ONE PERSON'S PROJECT ESTIMATE

Adding More Living Space

t's fun to imagine, but what might it actually cost to undertake a project described n this chapter? The example below describes a typical project and gives a general estimate of the costs involved.

Project Description

The addition of a 15 x 20 sq. ft. family room and the rehabilitation of the kitchen and powder room.

Architects' fees can be calculated in different ways. One way is to apply a percentage to all items that the architect designs, specifies and coordinates during construction. The following estimate is based on a percentage fee basis.

Family Room Addition

Traditionally detailed family room addition (300 sq. ft./$300 sq. ft.) $90,000
Exterior: brick and stone, classical frieze board, copper gutters and downspouts, cedar shingles or slate roofing.
Interior: 5/8-inch drywall with poplar base and crown moldings, herringbone clear oak flooring.
Entertainment cabinetry $10,000
Cherry rail-and-stile construction

Kitchen Rehab

Cabinetry, custom high-end $45,000
Appliances (built-in refrigerator, commercial grade equipment) $18,000
Stone countertops and backsplash $10,000
Plumbing, including fixtures $8,000
Electrical, including fixtures $6,000
Demolition and minimal construction $15,000
HVAC (heating, ventilating and air conditioning) $2,000

Powder Room Rehab

Cabinetry, custom high end $2,500
Stone countertops and tilework $5,000
Demolition and construction $3,000
Plumbing, including fixtures $7,000
Electrical, including fixtures $3,000

Sub Total **$224,500**
Contingency (10.00%) **$22,450**
Architectural fees (15.00%) **$33,675**

Total: **$280,625**

Note: Small additions cost more, on a square foot basis, than a large addition or a new house due

Built-in refrigerator,
Commercial grade
equipment

Custom
high-end
cabinetry

Stone
countertops
& backsplash

Architects

BUILT TO LAST

Custom home clients in North Carolina are abandoning the quest for the big house in favor of designing a home of high quality, integrity and harmonious balance. When the emphasis is on using top quality materials and custom design to create a comfortable home, the result is truly built to last.

TOO BIG, TOO SMALL, JUST RIGHT?

If you're designing rooms with dimensions different from what you're used to, get out the tape measure. If you're downsizing, can you fit the furniture into this space? Is the new, larger size big enough – or too big? Ask your architect, builder, or interior designer if there's a similar project you can visit to get a good feel for size.

• Ask lots of questions. Architects of luxury homes in the area are committed to providing their clients with information up front about the design process, the building process and their fees. These architects respect the sophistication and intelligence of their clientele, but do not necessarily expect them to have a high level of design experience or architectural expertise. Educating you is on their agenda.

• What is the breadth of services? Although this information is in your contract, it's important to know the level of services a firm will provide. There is no set standard and you need to be sure if an architect will provide the kind of services you want – from basic "no-frills" through "full service."

• Find out who you will be working with. Will you be working with one person or a team? Who will execute your drawings?

• Ask for references. Speak to past and current clients who built projects similar to yours. Ask for references from contractors with whom the architect works.

• Does the architect carry liability insurance?

• Ask to see examples of the architect's work – finished homes, job sites, and architectural plans. Does the work look and feel like what you want?

• Find out how many projects the architect has in progress. Will you get the attention you deserve?

• Decide if you like the architect. For successful collaboration, there must be a good personal connection. As you both suggest, reject, and refine ideas, a shared sense of humor and good communication will be what makes the process workable and enjoyable. Ask yourself, "Do I trust this person to deliver my dream and take care of business in the process?" If the answer is anything less than a strong and sure, "yes!" keep looking.

UNDERSTANDING ARCHITECTS' FEES AND CONTRACTS

Fees and fee structures vary greatly among architects, and comparing them can be confusing, even for the experienced client. Architects, like licensed professionals in other fields, are prohibited from setting fees as a group and agreeing on rates. They arrive at their fees based on:

(A) an hourly rate
(B) lump sum total
(C) percentage of construction cost
(D) dollars per square foot
(E) size of the job
(F) a combination of the above

The final quoted fee will include a set of services that may vary greatly from architect to architect. From a "no frills" to a "full service" bid, services are vastly different. For example, a no frills agreement budgets the architect's fee at two to seven percent of the construction cost; a full service contract budgets the architect's fee at 12 to 18 percent. Some firms include contractor's selection, bid procurement, field inspections, interior cabinetry, plumbing and lighting design, and punch list. Others don't.

One concrete basis for comparison is the architectural drawings. There can be a vast difference in the number of pages of drawings, the layers of drawings and the detail level of the specifications. Some include extra sketchbooks with drawings of all the construction details and in-depth written specs which call out every doorknob and fixture. Some offer impressive three-dimensional scale models to help you better visualize the end result, and computerized virtual walk throughs.

The benefit of a more detailed set of drawings is a more accurate, cost-effective construction bid. The more details noted in the drawings and text, the fewer contingencies a contractor will have to speculate on. The drawings are the sum total of what your contract with a builder is based upon. If a detail isn't included in the drawings, then it's not part of the project and you'll be billed extra for it.

Services should be clearly outlined in your contract. Many local architects use a standard American Institute of Architects (AIA) contract, in a long or short form. Some use a letter of agreement.

Have your attorney read the contract. Be clear that the level of service you desire is what the architect is prepared to deliver.

THE DESIGN PHASE

The architect will be in communication with you as your project progresses through the phases of schematic design, design development, preparation of construction documents, bidding and negotiating with a contractor, and contract administration (monitoring the construction). If any of these services will not be supplied, you should find out at your initial meeting.

The creativity belongs in the first phases. This is when you move walls, add windows, change your mind about the two-person whirlpool tub in favor of a shower surround, and see how far your budget will take you.

The time involved in the design process varies depending on the size of the project, your individual availability, and coordinating schedules.

WHY YOU SHOULD WORK WITH A TOP ARCHITECT

1. They are expert problem solvers. A talented architect can create solutions to your design problems, and solve the problems that stand in the way of achieving your dream.

2. They have creative ideas. You may see a two-story addition strictly in terms of its function – a great room with a master suite upstairs. An architect immediately applies a creative eye to the possibilities.

3. They provide a priceless product and service. A popular misconception about architects is that their fees make their services an extravagance. In reality, an architect's fee represents a small percentage of the overall building cost.

A good architect will encourage you to take as much time as you want in the first phases. It's not always easy to temper the euphoria that comes with starting to build a dream home, but the longer you live with the drawings, the happier you'll be. Spread the plans on a table and take an extra week or month to look at them.

Think practically. Consider what you don't like about your current home. If noise from the dishwasher bothers you at night, tell your architect you want a quiet bedroom, and a quiet dishwasher. Think about the nature of your future needs. Architects note that their clients are beginning to ask for "barrier-free" and ergonomic designs for more comfortable living as they age, or as their parents move in with them.

BUILDING BEGINS: BIDDING AND NEGOTIATION

If your contract includes it, your architect will bid your project to contractors he or she considers appropriate for your project, and any contractor you wish to consider. You may want to include a contractor to provide a "control" bid. If you wish to hire a specific contractor, you needn't go through the bidding process, unless you're simply curious about the range of responses you may receive. After the architect has analyzed the bids and the field is narrowed, you will want to meet the contractors to see if you're compatible, if you're able to communicate clearly, and if you sense a genuine interest in your project. These meetings can take place as a contractor walks through a home to be remodeled, or on a tour of a previously built project if you're building a new home.

If your plans come in over budget, the architect is responsible for bringing the costs down, except, of course, if the excess is caused by some item the architect had previously cautioned you would be prohibitive.

Not all people select an architect first. It's not uncommon for the builder to help in the selection of an architect, or for a builder to offer "design/build" services with architects on staff, just as an architectural firm may have interior designers on staff. ■

BUILDING GRAPHICS ARCHITECTURE ....(704) 542-1498
7400 Carmel Executive Park, Suite 150, Charlotte   Fax: (704) 542-1499
See Ad on Page: 78, 79, 90
Principal/Owner: Frank Snodgrass, Chris Boush, Kim Bunting
e-mail: dhlandi@yahoo.com

COMMUNITY PLANNING &
ARCHITECTURAL ASSOCIATES, LLC...(919) 489-1771
6330 Quadrangle Drive, Suite 260, Chapel Hill   Fax: (919) 489-3466
See Ad on Page: 98
Principal/Owner: Ralph Lasater
Website: www.cpaa-usa.com e-mail: rlasater@cpaa-usa.com

MEYER GREESON PAULIN..(704) 375-1001
320 S. Tryon Street, Suite 222, Charlotte   Fax: (704) 333-3620
See Ad on Page: 91
Principal/Owner: T. Mark Paullin, AIA
Website: www.mgparchitects.com e-mail: mark.paullin@mgparchitects.com
Additional Information: Meyer Greeson Paullin has established a design vocabulary
which allows it to reflect its clients' diverse needs and tastes along with a high
quality and depth of design.

MILLER ARCHITECTURE ....(704) 377-8500
360 North Caswell Road, Suite 200, Charlotte   Fax: (704) 377-8509
See Ad on Page: 92
Principal/Owner: Tony F. Miller, AIA
Website: www.millerarchitecture.com e-mail: tonymiller@millerarchitecture.com
Additional Information: For "something special" in architecture, fine home & estate
design renovations, multi-family design & millwork design.

PLANWORX ARCHITECTURE, PA...(919) 846-8100
5711 Six Forks Rd, Suite 100, Raleigh   Fax: (919) 846-2661
See Ad on Page: 80, 94, 95
Principal/Owner: Marc W. Mills and Ken Braswell
Website: www.planworx.com e-mail: info@planworx.com
Additional Information: Architectural firm serving the single and multi-family housing
industry with custom to stock plan product service.

SHAW/DAVIS ARCHITECTS, P.A. ....(919) 493-0528
114 Cricket Ground, Durham   Fax: (919) 490-0610
See Ad on Page: 96, 97
Principal/Owner: Keith Shaw AIA & Kevin Davis AIA
Website: www.shawdavis.com e-mail: Keith@shawdavis.com

STEVEN CLIPP ARCHITECTURE ....(919) 929-7838
22 Kendall Drive, Chapel Hill   Fax: (919) 929-7838
See Ad on Page: 93
Principal/Owner: Steven Clipp

89

320 South Tryon St. • Suite 222 • Charlotte, NC 28202
04) 375-1001 • Fax (704) 333-3620 • www.mgparchitects.cc

home *handcrafted*
Steven Clipp Architecture

Steven G. Clipp, AIA - Principal
22 Kendall Drive Chapel Hill North Carolina 27517 (919) 929 - 7838

Planworx | Architecture, P.A.

TAKE OUR PLANS *HOME.*

Planworx Architec

Naturally beautiful. Inviting exterior. Integrated elements. The home that invites you in. Dramatic spaces. Efficient planning. Bright openness. The home that accommodates your lifestyle. Planworx Architecture will guide you through the design process. Planworx has the professional expertise to uniquely and creatively design beyond your expectations. Our strong background in structural design, site design, multi-family and renovations makes Planworx a versatile residential group. Visit us at www.Planworx.com.

ture

SHAW/ DAVIS ARCHITECTS, P.A.

Keith Shaw, AIA
114 Cricket Ground
Durham, NC 27707
(919)493-0528
keith@shawdavis.com

Kevin Davis, AIA
102 Solitude Way
Cary, NC 27511
(919)233-4501
kevin@shawdavis.com

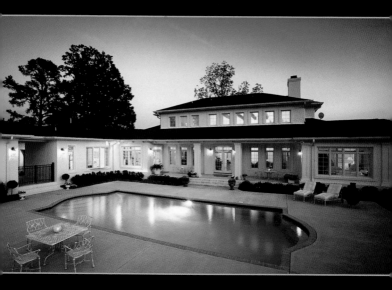

Award winning designers of custom luxury homes in North Carolina for over forty-three years.

Residential Designers

IMPEL INC. ....**(704) 366-7377**
7816 Fairview Road, Suite 301, Charlotte   Fax: (704) 366-7217
See Ad on Page: 109
Principal/Owner: Mirko Djuranovic
Website: www.impel-inc.com e-mail: mirko@impel-inc.com
Additional Information: We promote a concept of living. It is so different that after
you live in this house for a year or so, you can not imagine any other way of living.

NORTH DESIGN AND CONSTRUCTION ....**(828) 324-0500**
PO Box 717, Hickory   Fax: (828) 324-1708
See Ad on Page: 108, 132
Principal/Owner: G. Mark North

CHRISTOPHER PHELPS AND ASSOCIATES, LLC ....**(704) 377-5569**
428 East Fourth Street, Suite 310, Charlotte   Fax: (704) 377-6909
See Ad on Page: 112
Principal/Owner: Christoper Phelps
Website: www.christopherphelps.com
Additional Information: A residential design firm for individuals and builder's with
award winning homes in the Charlotte areas most prestigious neighborhoods.

DAVID THOMAS & ASSOCIATES INC. ....**(919) 870-5575**
6616-201 Six Forks Rd., Raleigh   Fax: (919) 870-7646
See Ad on Page: 110, 111
Principal/Owner: David Thomas
Website: e-mail: DTAdesign@aol.com
Additional Information: Designers of fine custom homes, interiors, landscapes,
renovations and restorations. Over 30 years experience.

WHJ DESIGN ....**(919) 489-4577**
P.O. Box 52015, Durham   Fax: (919) 419-0060
See Ad on Page: 113
Principal/Owner: Hutch Johnson
e-mail: whj@nc.rr.com

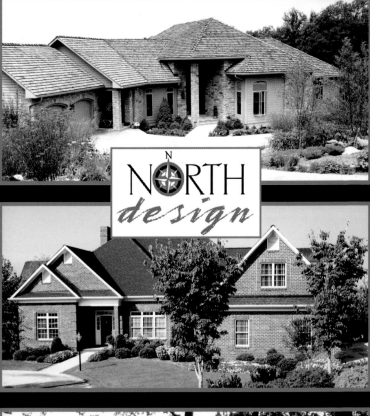

NORTH
design

HOME DESIGNS AND CONSTRUCTION
P.O. BOX 717, HICKORY, N.C. 28603-0717
828-324-0500

DAVID THOMAS
& ASSOCIATES INC.

6610-201 Six Forks Road, Raleigh, NC 27615

919-870-5575

DTAdesign@aol.com

Designers of Fine Custom Homes,
Interiors & Landscapes

- ◆ *Renovations / Restorations*
- ◆ *Interior Designers ASID & IIDA*
- ◆ *Over 30 Years Experience*

CHRISTOPHER PHELPS
& ASSOCIATES, LLC

a residential design firm

Homes designed

for the

art of living

W H J DESIGN, INC.

p.o. box 52015
durham, n.c. 27717
(919) 489-4577

Designers of fine quality
homes and renovations

Archi

SHARING
the Dream

What would you like in your dream home? A special bedroom suite for the family cat? An 8 ft. by 6 ft. aquarium? A basement pub with a dance floor? It's easy to visualize the parts. It can be a bit harder to envision the whole.

An architect can provide this vision by giving your dreams shape and putting them into three dimensions. Gifted architects can do even more than that.

A beautiful home such as this starts with a client verbalizing his or her desires to an architect who listens well.

Photo courtesy of **Planworx Architecture, P. A.**

itects

The hand-hewn natural stone fireplace, wood-planked ceiling, and touches of green enable the homeowner to celebrates the beauty of the outdoors inside.

Photo courtesy of **Meyer, Greeson, Paullin Architecture/Interior Design P.A.**
Photo by **JoAnn Sieburg-Baker**

During the "dream phase" or conceptual period of a project, they can help you assess the dynamics or soul of the house-the feeling and poetry that is unique to you and your family. This can make the difference between a house you like and a home you love. How do you most clearly communicate your personal dreams? Architects have many ways to help.

Some meet in a client's current home or walk the site of their new one. Others ask clients to show them pictures of homes or rooms they like. T. Mark Paullin, principal of Meyer, Greeson, Paullin Architecture/Interior Design P.A., thinks of these pictures as "psychological flashcards."

The one technique that all top architects agree on is listening. As Marc Mills, principal of Planworx Architecture, P.A., said, "Listening is key." Keith R. Shaw, principal of Shaw/Davis Architects, P.A. went a step further, "It's also important to be aware of the look on a client's face when a suggestion is made. It helps you understand what he or she is passionate about."

Top architects ask their clients to discuss likes, wants and dislikes, even if there are contradictions in the information given. "Sometimes I've been called a marriage counselor," said Frank Snodgrass, architect, Building Graphics.

Archi

Many architects have found that contradictions stimulate interesting design discussions and foster creative solutions. Paullin agrees, "It's all about compromise," he said. For example, when a female client envisioned an Old World interior with lots of stone and wood and her husband desired a more crisp, clean feel, Paullin pleased them both by adding a sleek, contemporary, lower-level entertainment room to the traditional home.

To encourage dialogue, Mills walks the home site, as does Snodgrass. Shaw gives his clients a questionnaire with a list of rooms and an accompanying list of adjectives with which to describe them.

A client's likes are essential to know, but their dislikes are important as well. While chatting with a client, Paullin discovered that this homeowner disliked seeing his wife's open closet door. Paullin's solution was to design his and hers closets far enough apart that one never had to look at the other's.

Shaw sees himself as a bit of a design detective. "In order to make the home flow in a way that makes both their lives comfortable," he said, "I ask a number of questions. Like who likes to read before going to bed, which one gets up first in the morning and what do they do once they get out of bed?" This lifestyle line of questioning can affect the design of a new home in a positive way.

More than just an envelope for living, this great room, with its abundance of light and use of natural materials, captures the spirit of the homeowner.

Photo courtesy of **Shaw/Davis Architects, P.A.**
Photo by **Seth Tice-Lewis**

itects

Even the most formal home can achieve an informal look through the correct placement of light and color.

Photo courtesy of Planworx Architecture, P.A.

For a client who liked to stay up late and read, Paullin created a separate room in the master bedroom. He designed it with a pocket door that closed it off from the cozy sleeping chamber. When another client wanted dinner guests to feel comfortable in their secluded, vacation home deep in the woods, Shaw designed an internal dining room without windows.

Archi

An architect's creativity and ingenuity can overcome many obstacles. For a client who didn't want lights in his dining room ceiling, Shaw created an impressive, fiber optic ceiling. Paullin's client mentioned that it would be nice if he could swim from his inside workout room right into his outdoor pool. Even though construction was completed when the client made his request, Paullin found a way to make it happen.

tects

To a top architect, everything a client cares about is important, no matter how small or large. Snodgrass designed a massive 8 ft. by 6 ft. aquarium as a serene environment for a leading professional race car driver. He also created a full pub, complete with dance floor, as a background for another client's German beer stein collection. For an animal lover, Mills designed a pet-pleasing bedroom suite for the homeowners cat.

To enhance their client's lifestyles, these architects have designed wine cellars with vaulted ceilings and working gaslights. They've recreated architectural styles that reflected their clients' world travels. And they've designed special areas for family heirlooms.

Today's top architects are ever aware of things that many clients often don't consider. A good architect will be sensitive to the unique qualities of the environment that might impact the design of a new home: where the sun comes up, the direction the wind blows, the look of the natural environment and the topography. Architects also consider changes in the family dynamic and design homes that can adapt as children grow or as couples face the "empty nest."

The feeling and poetry engendered by the style of a residence can make the difference between a home you like and a home you love.

Photo courtesy of **Meyer, Greeson, Paullin Architecture/Interior Design P.A.**
Photo by **JoAnn Sieburg-Baker**

Archi

Lifestyle desires can be satisfied while maintaining the architectural integrity of a residence.

Photo courtesy of **Shaw/Davis Architects, P.A.**
Photo by **Charles Register**

As your dreams begin to take shape, your architect will have countless ways to help you visualize his or her ideas, even in the earliest conceptual meetings. Many sketch ideas as they are verbalized. Some use 3-D computer imagery that allows clients to virtually walk from room to room in a home that is still in the dream stage. For clients who have trouble looking at a two-dimensional plan and imagining it in three dimensions, Snodgrass sometimes illustrates size by using rooms and pieces of furniture in his office. For instance, his conference room table is 8 ft. by 4 ft.-just about the dimensions of a kitchen island. But even during the construction process, size relationships can fool people.

Snodgrass told the story of a client who called him in tears. She had just been out to look at the foundation of her new house. When she saw the hole in the in the middle of the ground, she was certain her grand house has shrunk to the size of a bungalow. Snodgrass assured her that her home was exactly the right size and that the spatial relationship of the foundation to the large lot had fooled her. And sure enough, when her home was framed, then built, it was, indeed, the size she thought it would be.

Never be shy about sharing visions with your architect. This sharing is the door to a collaboration that can be enjoyable and fruitful. You'll find that an architect is dedicated to shaping your dream and making it come true. And it will. ■

itects

Finally...
North Carolina's Own
Home & Design
Sourcebook

The **North Carolina Home Book** is your final destination when searching for home remodeling, building and decorating resources. This comprehensive, hands-on sourcebook to building, remodeling, decorating, furnishing, and landscaping a luxury home is required reading for the serious and discriminating homeowner. With more than 500 full-color, beautiful pages, the **North Carolina Home Book** is the most complete and well-organized reference to the home industry. This hardcover volume covers all aspects of the process, includes listings of hundreds of industry professionals, and is accompanied by informative and valuable editorial discussing the most recent trends. Ordering your copy of the **North Carolina Home Book** now can ensure that you have the blueprints to your dream home, in your hand, today.

Order your copy now!

Published by
The Ashley Group
8420 University Executive
Suite 810
Charlotte, NC 28262
704.549.3687 fax: 704.549.3695
E-mail: ashleybooksales@cahners.com

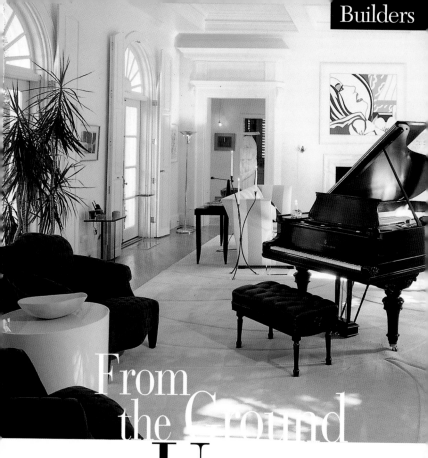

From the Ground Up

One of the key players in every homebuilding and remodeling success story is the builder. Architects envision possibilities, but builders create new realities. While design/build teams of architects and builders are becoming increasingly popular, the home in which you will be living will be the direct result of your contractor's efforts and expertise. So much of your satisfaction in the final outcome depends upon the selection of the right builder. It is essential to choose a company or individual with whom you have a good rapport, who has excellent references as well as experience with your type of project. While the planning phase of a new home or remodeling project may be exciting, creating the finished product is hard work. Seek out a builder whose attention to quality detail, willingness to listen to your concerns, and in-depth knowledge of the trades assures you a smoother road on the way to your new home.

Photo courtesy of **Swimmer Construction**

THE TEARDOWN TREND

Land for new residential construction is getting harder to find, and "tear-down" renovations are becoming more common. There are often mixed emotions in an existing neighborhood as old structures come down. If you are considering a "tear-down" property, be sure you work with a builder and architect who are sensitive to the character of the neighborhood, and will help you build a home that fits in.

SETTING THE STANDARD FOR QUALITY

A strong commitment to providing top quality materials and craftsmanship is the most important contribution a builder can make to your professional team. Working in concert with your architect, interior designer, kitchen and bath designer and landscape architect, a custom home builder will take the designs, and your dreams, and make them happen. Selecting a builder who shares your dedication to building only the best is how you build quality into your new home. This kind of quality is as tangible as it is intangible. You can see it in the materials used – not necessarily the most expensive, but always the best for the situation. More interestingly, you can feel it. There's an unmistakable sense of integrity in a well-built home, of a dream fulfilled.

IS IT A(ARCHITECT) BEFORE B(BUILDER) OR B BEFORE A?

Answering this question can seem like the "chicken or the egg" riddle: Do you hire the builder first, the architect first, or choose a design/build firm, where both functions are under the same roof?

If you work first with an architect, his or her firm will recommend builders they know who have a track record in building homes of the same caliber you desire. Most likely, your architect contract will include bidding and negotiation services with these builders, and you may expect help in analyzing bids and making your selection. Your architect contract also may include construction administration, in which the architect makes site visits to observe construction, reviews the builder's applications for payment, and helps make sure the home is built according to the plans.

Perhaps you've seen previous work or know satisfied clients of a custom home builder, and wish to work with him. In this scenario, the builder will recommend architects who are experienced in successfully designing homes and/or additions similar to what you want. The builder will support you, and the architect will cost-control information through realistic cost figures, before products are integrated into the house.

If you like the idea of working with one firm for both the architectural design and building, consider a design/build firm. Design/build firms offer an arrangement that can improve time management and efficient communication, simply by virtue of having both professional functions under the same roof. There is also added flexibility as the project develops. If you decide you want to add a feature, the design/build firm handles the design process and communicates the changes internally to the builder. When you interview a design/builder firm, it's important to ascertain that the firm has a strong architectural background, with experienced custom home architects on staff.

All scenarios work and no one way is always better than the other. Make your choice by finding professionals you trust and with whom you feel comfortable. Look for vision and integrity and let the creative process begin.

FINDING THE RIGHT BUILDER

The selection of a builder or remodeler is a major decision, and should be approached in a thoughtful, unhurried manner. Allow plenty of time to interview and research at least two candidates before making your choice. Hours invested at this point can save months of time later on.

At the initial interview, the most important information you'll get is not from brochures, portfolios, or a sales pitch, but from your own intuition. Ask yourself: Can we trust this person to execute plans for our dream home, likely the biggest expenditure of our lifetime? Is there a natural two-way communication, mutual respect, and creative energy? Does he have the vision to make our home unique and important? Is his sense of the project similar to ours? Will we have any fun together? Can we work together for at least a year?

If you answer "Yes!" you've found the most valuable asset – the right chemistry.

TAKE TIME TO CHECK REFERENCES

The most distinguished builders in the area expect, even want, you to check their references. More luxury home clients are taking the time to do this research as the move toward quality workmanship continues to grow.

Talk to clients. Get a list of clients spanning the last three to five years, some of whom are owners of projects similar to yours. Call them and go visit their homes or building sites. Satisfied customers are only too happy to show you around and praise the builder who did the work. If you can, speak with a past client not on the builder's referral list. Finding one unhappy customer is not cause for concern, but if you unearth a number of them, cross that builder off your list.

Visit a construction site. Clients who get the best results appreciate the importance of the subcontractors. Their commitment to quality is at the heart of the job. Do the subcontractors appear to be professional? Are they taking their time in doing their work? Is the site clean and neat?

TEN GOOD QUESTIONS TO ASK A BUILDER'S PAST CLIENTS

1. Are you happy with your home?
2. Was the house built on schedule?
3. Did the builder respect the budget and give an honest appraisal of costs early on?
4. Did the builder bring creativity to your project?
5. Were you well informed so you properly understood each phase of the project?
6. Was the builder accessible and on-site?
7. Does the builder provide good service now that the project is complete?
8. How much help did you get from the builder in choosing the products in your home?
9. Is the house well built?
10. Would you hire the builder again?

121

IT TAKES HOW LONG?

Some typical construction time frames:

Total Kitchen Remodel: From total demolition to installation of new cabinets, flooring, appliances, electrical, etc. SIX – EIGHT WEEKS

A 1,400 Sq. Ft. Addition: New first floor Great Room & powder room, extension of the existing kitchen; master suite upstairs. FOUR – SIX MONTHS

Total Home Remodel: An 1,800 sq. ft. Colonial expanded to 4,000 sq. ft. All spaces redefined, added third floor, three new baths, new high-end kitchen, deck. SIX - NINE MONTHS

These estimates depend on factors such as the size of the crew working on your project, the timeliness of decisions and the delivery of materials.

Contact subcontractors with whom the builder has worked. If they vouch for the builder's integrity and ability, you'll know the firm has earned a good professional reputation. Meeting subcontractors also provides a good measure for the quality of workmanship you'll receive.

Visit the builder's office. Is it well-staffed and organized? Does this person offer the technology for virtual walk-throughs? Do you feel welcome there?

Find out how long the builder has been in business. Experienced custom builders have strong relationships with top quality subcontractors and architects, a comprehensive knowledge of products and materials, and skills to provide the best service before, during and after construction.

Ask how many homes are currently being built and how your project will be serviced. Some builders work on several homes at once; some limit their total to 10 or 12 a year.

LAYING A FOUNDATION FOR SUCCESS

Two documents, the contract and the timeline, define your building experience. The contract lays down the requirements of the relationship and the timeline delineates the order in which the work is done. While the contract is negotiated once at the beginning of the relationship, the timeline continues to be updated and revised as the project develops.

THE CONTRACT

The American Institute of Architects (AIA) provides a standard neutral contract which is widely used in the area, but some firms write their own contracts. As with any contract, get legal advice, read carefully, and assume nothing. If landscaping is not mentioned, then landscaping will not be provided. Pay careful attention to:

• Payment schedules. When and how does the builder get paid? How much is the deposit (depends on the total cost of the project but $10,000 to $25,000 is not uncommon) and will it be applied against the first phase of the work? Do you have the right to withhold any payment until your punch list is completed? Will you write checks to the builder (if so, insist on sworn waivers) or only to the title company? Remodeling contracts typically use a payment schedule broken into thirds – one-third up front, one-third half-way through the project, and one-third at completion. You may withhold a negotiated percentage of the contract price until you're satisfied that the terms of the contract have been met and the work has been inspected.

This should be stipulated in the contract. Ten percent is the average amount to be held back, but is negotiable based on the overall size of the project.

Builders and remodeling specialists who attract a quality-minded, high-end custom home client are contacted by institutions offering attractive construction or bridge and end loan packages. Ask your contractor for referrals if you want to do some comparative shopping.

• The total cost-breakdown of labor and materials expenses.

• Change order procedures. Change orders on the average add seven to ten percent to the cost of a custom home. Be clear on how these orders are charged and the impact they eventually will have on the timetable.

• The basic work description. This should be extremely detailed, including everything from installing phone jacks to the final cleaning of your home. A comprehensive list of specified materials should be given, if it hasn't already been provided by your architect.

• Allowances. Are they realistic? This is one place where discrepancies will be evident. Is Contractor A estimating $75,000 for cabinets while Contractor B is stating $150,000?

• Warranty. A one-year warranty, effective the date you move in, is standard in this area.

THE TIMELINE

This changeable document will give you a good indication if and when things will go wrong.

Go to the site often enough to keep track of the progress according to the timeline. Do what you need to do to keep the project on schedule. One of the main causes of delays and problems is late decision-making by the homeowner. If you wait until three weeks prior to cabinet installation to order your cabinets, you can count on holding up the entire process by at least a month. (You'll also limit your options to cabinets that can be delivered quickly.)

THE SECOND TIME'S A CHARM

Renovating a home offers the unique excitement of reinventing an old space to serve a new, enhanced purpose. It's an evolutionary process, charged with creative thinking and bold ideas. If you enjoy a stimulating environment of problem solving and decision making, and you're prepared to dedicate the needed time and resources, remodeling

TRUTH ABOUT CHANGE ORDERS

The building process demands an environment that allows for changes as plans move from paper to reality. Although you can control changes through careful planning in the preliminary stages of design and bidding, budget an extra seven to 10 percent of the cost of the home to cover change orders. Changes are made by talking to the contractor, not someone working at the site. You will be issued a change order form, which you will sign and return to the contractor. Keep your copies of the forms together in one folder. Avoid last minute sticker shock by being diligent in keeping a current tab on your change order expenses.

One Person's Project Estimate:

Creating a Custom Home

It's fun to imagine, but what might it actually cost to undertake a project described in this chapter? The example below describes a typical project and gives a general estimate of the costs involved.

Project Description

Construction of a 10,000 sq. ft., country-style home with brick and stone veneer and a slate roof.

Rough Lumber and Exterior Trim	Exterior	$15,000
	Rough framing	$95,000
Carpentry	Caulking	$2,000
	Rough framing	$90,000
	Interior trim	$12,000
Steel and Ornamental Iron	Ornamental iron	$5,000
	Structural steel	$7,500
Windows	Skylight	$1,500
	Windows and doors	$75,000
Exterior Doors	Front door	$12,000
	Service door	$2,500
Roof	Slate	$140,000
Plumbing	Fixtures	$25,000
	Labor	$25,000
Heating	HVAC forced air	$45,000
	Radiant heat	$12,500
Electrical	Electrical	$50,000
	Security system	$5,000
Masonry Veneer		$215,000
Insulation		$10,000
Drywall		$38,000
Wood Floors		$30,000
Tile	Ceramic tile	$30,000
	Hearth and surround	$10,500
Cabinets and Vanities		$125,000
Interior Trim	Mantel	$10,900
	Wine rack	$3,000
	Closets	$8,000
Shower Doors and Tub Enclosure		$9,000
Gutters and Downspouts		$13,000
Garage Doors and Opener		$4,800

Total: **$1,147,200**

Note: This estimate covers the basic construction costs of the project. Other costs include insurance and legal fees, survey and site plans, grading, light fixtures and appliance installation, and clean up of the site.

Rough cut
siding

Stone
veneer

Slate
roof

will result in a home which lives up to all of your expectations. You'll be living in the neighborhood you love, in a home that fits your needs.

A WORD ABOUT FINANCING OF REMODELING PROJECTS

Payment schedules in remodeling contracts typically require a deposit or a first payment at the start of the project, with subsequent payments due monthly or in conjunction with the progress of the work.

It is within your rights to withhold a negotiated percentage of the contract price until you're satisfied that the terms of the contract have been met and the work has been inspected. This should be stipulated in the written contract. Ten percent is the average amount to be held back, but is negotiated based on the overall size of the project.

Remodeling specialists who attract a quality-minded clientele are kept abreast of the most attractive remodeling loans on the market by lenders who specialize in these products. Ask your remodeler for referrals to these financial institutions.

UPDATING THE CLASSICS

Many homeowners at the beginning of the new century are attracted to the historic architecture in older neighborhoods. Maturity and classicism are factors that persuade homeowners to make an investment in an old home and restore, renovate or preserve it, depending on what level of involvement interests them and the significance of the house. Renovations include additions and updating or replacing systems in the house. Restorations involve restoring the building to the specifications original to the house. Preservation efforts preserve what's there.

Like any remodeling project, it's an emotional and personal experience, only more so. Staying within the confines of a certain period or style is difficult and time consuming. That's why it's crucial to find an experienced architect and builder who share a reverence for tradition and craftsmanship. At your interview, determine if his or her portfolio shows competence in this specialty. It's vital to find a professional who understands historic projects and knows experienced and qualified contractors and/or subcontractors who will do the work for you. Ask if he or she knows experienced contractors who work in historic districts and have relationships with knowledgeable, experienced craftsmen. If you want exterior features, like period gardens or terraces, ask

SOURCE FOR HISTORIC PROPERTIES

The National Trust for Historic Preservation 1785 Massachusetts Avenue, N.W. Washington, D.C. 20036 (202) 588-6000

Having a home listed on the National Register doesn't restrict homeowners from demolishing or making changes (local restrictions do that), but offers possible financial assistance and tax credits for renovations, and limited protection against federal "takings." The organization sponsors programs, publishes newsletters and books, and advocates preservation.

Local foundations and historical societies are established in most of the North Carolina communities that have older homes.

if they will be included in the overall plan. Make sure he or she has sources for you to find period furnishings, sconce shades or chimney pots.

There are many construction and design issues particular to old homes. The historic renovation and preservation experts featured in the following pages bring experience, creativity and responsibility to each project.

RESPECT YOUR ELDERS

Before you fall in love with an old house, get a professional opinion. Find out how much is salvageable before you make the investment. Can the wood be restored? Have the casings been painted too many times? Is the plaster wavy and buckled? Can the house support ductwork for central air conditioning or additional light sources?

Notable remodelers are often contacted for their expert advice prior to a real estate purchase, and realtors maintain relationships with qualified remodelers for this purpose. They also keep remodelers informed of special properties suitable for custom renovations as they become available.

PRIVACY? WHAT'S THAT?

Remodelers overwhelmingly agree their clients are happier if they move to a temporary residence during all, or the most intensive part, of the renovation. The sight of the roof and walls being torn out, the constant banging and buzzing of tools, and the invasion of privacy quickly take their toll on children and adults who are trying to carry on family life in a house full of dust. Homeowners who are well-rested from living in clean, well-lighted temporary quarters enjoy better relationships with each other, their remodeler and subcontractors.

Common hideaways are rental homes, suite-type hotels, the unoccupied home of a relative, or a long vacation trip. ■

A LUXURY ADDITION OF AN HISTORIC HOME

Suburban Arts and Crafts-Prairie Home, circa 1915.
• All windows, trim, casings and other details to match the original brick.
• Full, finished basement, with bar and workout area.
• First level family room, dining room and new kitchen.
• Upper level master suite and office. Stone terrace and garden.

Total Project Cost: $500,000, including architectural fees.

127

CHIOTT CUSTOM HOMES, INC. ....**(704) 333-6055**
1108 East Boulevard, Charlotte
Fax: (704) 333-6056
See Ad on Page: 129
<u>Principal/Owner:</u> D. Jonathan Chiott

DIENST CUSTOM HOMES ....**(704) 892-8426**
19315 West Catawba Avenue, Suite 200, Cornelius
Fax: (704) 896-5876
See Ad on Page: 116, 117, 130, 131
<u>Principal/Owner:</u> Jocelyn Dienst
<u>Website:</u> www.diensthomes.com <u>e-mail:</u> jdienst@diensthomes.com
<u>Additional Information:</u> Since 1985, Dienst has built its reputation on state-of-the-art construction technology, craftsmanship, superior building products, and attention to detail.

GARY JOBE BUILDER, INC. ....**(336) 272-2772**
421 N. Edgeworth Street, Greensboro
Fax: (336) 274-5123
See Ad on Page: 178, 179
<u>Principal/Owner:</u> Gary Jobe
<u>e-mail:</u> garyjobebuilder@triad.rr.com

MEADOWS CUSTOM HOMEBUILDERS ....**(919) 781-3438**
12339-110 Wake Union Church Rd., Wake Forest
Fax: (919) 781-0676
See Ad on Page: 164
<u>Principal/Owner:</u> R. Dwayne Meadows
<u>e-mail:</u> dmeadows@pointswestnc.com
<u>Additional Information:</u> Building your American Dream.

NORTH DESIGN AND CONSTRUCTION ....**(828) 324-0500**
PO Box 717, Hickory
Fax: (828) 324-1708
See Ad on Page: 108, 132
<u>Principal/Owner:</u> G. Mark North

PFAHL CUSTOM BUILDERS, INC. ....**(704) 342-1065**
1200 The Plaza, Suite E, Charlotte
Fax: (704) 342-1093
See Ad on Page: 176
<u>Principal/Owner:</u> Kevin & Susan Pfahl
<u>Website:</u> www.pfahl.com <u>e-mail:</u> susan@pfahl.com
<u>Additional Information:</u> Providing architectural and construction services including custom homes, historic renovation, additions and remodeling.

REGAL CUSTOM HOME BUILDERS, LLC ....**(704) 243-0570**
PO Box 2669, Matthews
Fax: (704) 243-0575
See Ad on Page: 148, 149
<u>Principal/Owner:</u> Brian Spiers
<u>Website:</u> www.regalchb.com <u>e-mail:</u> mdspiers@mindspring.com

RUFTY HOMES, INC. ....**(919) 460-8550**
107 Edinburgh Drive South, Suite 146 , Cary
Fax: (919) 460-5756
See Ad on Page: 118, 160, 161
<u>Principal/Owner:</u> John Rufty
<u>Website:</u> www.rufty.com <u>e-mail:</u> jon@rufty.com

128

continued on page **141**

© Pat Shanklin

© Michael LoBiondo

© Michael LoBiondo

Building in Charlotte's finest neighborhoods, on your lot or ours.

CHIOTT
CUSTOM HOMES, INC.

1108 East Boulevard ◆ Charlotte, NC 28203 ◆ 704-333-6055

DIENST
Custom Homes

Experience the Dienst Difference

19315 West Catawba Avenue, Suite 200 • Cornelius, North Carolina 28031

Tel: 704.892.8426 • Fax: 704.896.5876

www.diensthomes.com

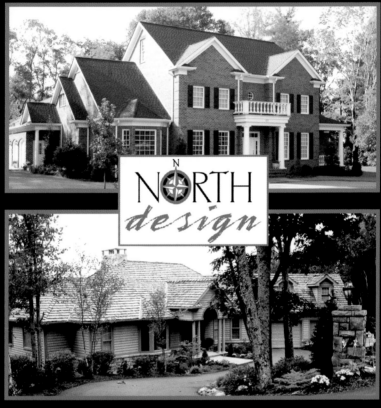

NORTH
design

HOME DESIGNS AND CONSTRUCTION
P.O. BOX 717, HICKORY, N.C. 28603-0717
828-324-0500

DAVID SIMONINI
Custom Homes, Inc.

501 East Morehead Street, Suite 4
Charlotte, NC 28202
704-334-6455
www.davidsimonini.com

A New Tradition of

Building Excellence

Unique, architecturally correct masterpieces...
Attention to detail...Unsurpassed customer service.
n a word, "Perfection." David Simonini Custom Home
s the premier custom homebuilder in the Charlotte are;
We work with our homeowners from the design of
the home's floor plan to the selection of interior and
exterior features. Contact us today to begin
working on your dream home.

DAVID SIMONINI
Custom Homes, Inc.

501 East Morehead Street, Suite 4
Charlotte, NC 28202
704-334-6455
www.davidsimonini.com

continued from page **128**

DAVID SIMONINI CUSTOM HOMES, INC. ....**(704) 334-6455**
501 East Morehead Street, Suite 4, Charlotte   Fax: (704) 334-6123
See Ad on Page: 133, 134, 135, 136, 137, 138, 139,
Principal/Owner: David Simonini
Website: www.davidsimonini.com   e-mail: davidsimonini@davidsimonini.com
Additional Information: Architecturally correct masterpieces... Attention to detail...
Unsurpassed customer service. In a word, "Perfection". Contact David Simonini
Custom Homes to begin working on your dream home.

DENNIS SOSEBEE CUSTOM HOMES, INC. ....**(336) 288-1072**
PO Box 38723, Greensboro   Fax: (336) 288-6019
See Ad on Page: 180, 181
Principal/Owner: Dennis L. Sosebee
e-mail: dezach@msn.com
Additional Information: In the past six years Dennis Sosebee has experienced sales
growth from $400,000 to $10,000,000.

SOUTHERN STRUCTURES, INC. ....**(336) 292-6774**
PO Box 19348, Greensboro   Fax: (336) 292-3013
See Ad on Page: 174, 175
Principal/Owner: Martha Faw
e-mail: mfaw01@aol.com
Additional Information: Southern Structures has built a quality reputation over the
past 20 years throughout the Triad by offering "Custom First — Quality First" custom
homes as a standard feature —— not an option.

SPECIALTY BUILDER, INC. ....**(919) 562-6912**
P.O. Box 1658, Wake Forest   Fax: (919) 562-6913
See Ad on Page: 146, 147
Principal/Owner: Richard M. Kolarov
Website: www.specialtybuilder.com   e-mail: specialitybuilder@mindspring.com
Additional Information: Experienced personal attention during the construction
of your luxury home.

SUNSTAR HOMES, INC. ....**(336) 286-4790**
2904 Lawndale Dr./PO Box 9696, Greensboro   Fax: (336) 286-5343
e-mail: allensunstar@aol.com

141

PHILIP D. THOMAS CUSTOM HOMES INC. ....**(336) 282-7261**
PO Box 38156, Greensboro   Fax: (336) 282-1715
See Ad on Page: 158, 159
Principal/Owner: Philip D. Thomas

continued on page **173**

UNIQUE HOMES
of Charlotte INC.

More than a home "An original work of art"

Dreaming
Creativity
Design
Pride
Commitment
Integrity
Innovation
"Hands On"

Architectural
Elements

Cost Benefit
Analysis

Remarkable
and
Unmistakable
Excellence

UNIQUE HOMES

*I'm not famous...
but, my homes are!*

UNIQUE HOMES
of Charlotte INC.

*Unique Homes
inspires you to
share in our
passion for*

7621 Little Ave., Suite 201
Charlotte, NC 28226
P 704-341-3390 •
D 704-995-3330

UNIQUE HOMES
of Charlotte INC.

7621 Little Ave., Suite 201 Charlotte, NC 28226
Phone: 704-341-3390 • Direct: 704-995-3330

luxury
craftsmanship
sophistication

Three ideas. One source.

SPECIALTY
BUILDER
INCORPORATED

Richard Kolarov/Master Builder (919) 562-6912
E-mail: *specialtybuilder@mindspring.com*
On the web: *www.specialtybuilder.com*

Regal Custom Homes LLC

P.O. Box 2669

Matthews, NC 28106

704-243-0570 office

704-243-0575 fax

HomeB

DETAILING
the Dream

W hile architects interpret dreams, custom home builders make them reality. Their prodigious talents have created exquisite homes, true showcases for the lifestyles of their owners. Since these gifted builders have constructed homes in many different architectural styles, the Home Book asked four of North Carolina's top custom builders to imagine their own dream home. If the sky was the limit and they could chose a site anywhere in the world, where would they build their dream home, and what would it be like?

151

Jocelyn Dienst, of Dienst Custom Homes, favors a media room such as this, with comfortable furniture, a bar and easy access to the outside.

Photo courtesy of **Dienst Custom Homes**
Photo by **Tim Buchman**

uilders

Not surprisingly, the responses were as varied as were the lifestyles of the custom builders themselves.

Jocelyn Dienst, principal of Dienst Custom Homes, has two grown children and a large extended family of avid skiers, rock climbers and bicycle enthusiasts. Since she would like to build a home that they would love to visit often, Dienst chose a site in the Colorado Mountains.

Rustic but elegant, her dream home would look like a spectacular Sun Valley lodge. Designed with many windows for a panoramic view of the mountains, it would be constructed of natural, rounded stones in various sizes. In front, a large rock fountain would greet guests.

Once beyond a covered entry made from large timbers, her guests would pass through a 9 ft. high mahogany and leaded glass entrance door. Inside, they'd find themselves in a large combination great room and dining room. Designed for family gatherings, it would feature heart of pine floors and high, tongue-in-groove wood ceilings enhanced with rustic, open rafters.

The dining area of the room would feature a table big enough to seat the entire family. A dramatic, 20 ft. fireplace would serve as a focal point and family gathering place. Textured and faux finished, the walls would enhance the rustic look of the home, and interior wood would be stained to best show off its natural beauty.

Dienst loves fireplaces and her dream home would have many. Along with the spectacular fireplace in the great room, there would be fireplaces in the family hearth room, the bedrooms and the state-of-the-art kitchen. Graced with glass-doored, natural pine cabinets, granite countertops and a matte multicolored natural slate floor, her dream kitchen would also boast a windowed breakfast room with mountain views. To round off the angles in a room, Deinst often uses turned columns in the corners of the room, and her dream home kitchen would feature them as well.

Deinst would have a number of second floor guestrooms, and because she'd like her parents to visit often, she'd also install an elevator. Designed for entertaining and relaxing, her media room wouldn't have theater seating. Instead, you'd find comfortable furniture, a bar and serving area, and easy access to an outside heated pool.

Bruce L. Bleiman, president of Unique Homes of Charlotte, Inc., couldn't chose between dream homes, so he opted to build two, each in a different geographical area. "They would be my own private resorts, spas and country clubs," he said.

Because his entire family skis, and he has loved the area since he first visited in his teens, Bleiman would construct his first home on the edge of a mountain overlooking beautiful Lake Tahoe. At the end of a tumbled stone

An ideal blending of period style and relaxed comfort, this library is the perfect place to unwind or receive friends.

Photo courtesy of **Dienst Custom Homes**
Photo by **Tim Buchman**

uilders

Warm colors can make even the largest and grandest homes seem welcoming.

Photo courtesy of **Dienst Custom Homes**
Photo by **Tim Buchman**

154

HomeB

drive, beyond a sparkling fountain in the center of a large turnaround, you'd come upon an English Country manor carved into the lush Nevada countryside.

Constructed of heavy boulder stones with sharp, jagged edges, the grand home would have a rustic flair.
It would also feature a glass-paneled, copper framed conservatory that he would use as a sunroom or an intimate entertainment area.

The interior of the main house would boast 24 ft. high ceilings, 10 ft. doors, a floating elliptical stairway and many windows, each capturing a fabulous view. Bleiman's 22 ft. by 36 ft. formal grand room would feature a coffered ceiling and a massive but elegant fireplace with a hand-carved, limestone surround. His library would boast an abundance of mahogany, highly finished like a piece of fine antique furniture. His dream home would also have a number of guest suites.

Because his dream house would be part spa, Bleiman would create a separate spa wing. Here, family and guests would discover an indoor mineral bath pool. A nearby therapy room would include a 10 ft. by 10 ft. sauna and a matching steam room. He would install a state-of-the-art music system and specially designed lighting to create a calm, relaxing mood. His spa wing would also contain massage rooms with a gentle waterfall feature in each, as well as an 'after therapy' area with oversize leather chairs and ottomans, a large plasma television and books.

Bleiman's second dream home would be situated on the ocean in South Florida. The sprawling, Mediterranean-style home would be built with two courtyards. The large, inner courtyard would be lushly landscaped and enhanced with terra cotta tile, an outdoor fireplace and an exuberant fountain. A smaller, more private courtyard off the master bath would feature an outdoor tub and shower.

Bleiman's South Florida home would also have a spa with many of the same amenities as he envisioned in his Colorado home. However, this separate spa area would also feature retractable doors to the outdoor pool and an arched loggia.

Custom homebuilder Richard Kolarov, principal of Specialty Builder, Inc., builds large, luxury Colonial style homes, but his dream home wouldn't be at all like those he builds. Since he and his wife are nearing the time when the children will be grown and out of the house, Kolarov would reward himself with a cozy, 1 1/2 story stone and timber home at the top of a heavily wooded mountain.

uilders

Even in the most classically styled residence, a homeowner's modern lifestyle desires can be satisfied with elegance and grace.

Photo courtesy of **Dienst Custom Homes**
Photo by **Tim Buchman**

Kolarov would place his home at the end of a long, secluded gravel road, on a home site that would overlook a clear mountain lake. This home would provide an environment where he and his wife could escape the outside world if they wished. It would also be a place where Kolarov could enjoy the outdoor activities he loves. There would be no cable TV, no Internet connection and no fax machine. The couple owns two Labrador retrievers, and this would be a house where they would always be welcome.

Upon entering the home, you would feel like you had just stepped into a European cottage. Native pine would cover the floors and exposed, reclaimed wood beams would give the ceilings a look of permanence and age. His comfortable gathering room would have a large fireplace as its focus. Muted fall colors, like rusts and browns, would cover the comfortable, soft furniture.

The master bedroom would have a separate sitting area and fireplace with access to an attached porch. The master bathroom would contain a waterfall-like shower that would cascade off the surrounding natural rock walls. Upstairs in the loft area he would construct a guest suite.

As these builders demonstrate, with thought and vision, dreams can become reality and fantasies can come true...even yours. ■

HomeB

157

With some thought and vision, anyone's dream home can become a reality.

Photo courtesy of **Dienst Custom Homes**
Photo by **Tim Buchman**

uilders

Philip D. Thomas

Custom Homes

(336) 282-7261

P.O. Box 38156 • Greensboro, NC 27438-8156

www.PhilipDThomas.com

Rufty
HOMES

The leading custom home
builder in the Central Carolinas –

where each home becomes a
beautiful composition.

WOLFE **W** HOMES

Beautiful memories. Custom made.

www.wolfehomes.net

Jim Wolfe & David Schenck, Greensboro, NC
336-299-2969

MEADOWS CUSTOM BUILDERS

5816 CREEDMOOR RD., SUITE 210 • RALEIGH, NC 27612
OFFICE (919) 781-3438 • FAX (919) 781-0676

Building Your **Dream** Home

T his timetable is included to support you in transforming your dream into reality. The sections of this book include specific categories to help you find the best quality craftsmanship available. This timeline will help you to understand the process from start to finish. How long might it take for you from designing the house to making it your own home? It could take from one year to a year and a half. Eighteen months is not unusual for a completely custom-built home. It can take four to six months to receive design approval and city permits alone. So be patient and plan ahead. Often delays occur because of a lack of communication. Take the initiative to keep in touch with all parties necessary. We hope this timeline will help give you an indication of how that dream home of yours will become a reality!

Project
Description

Building an upscale, one-acre property, single-family home. This work includes planning the project (selecting an architect and builder), executing the project (the steps from breaking the ground to finishing the interior work) and finishing the project (closing on your new home).

In Conclusion

Your new house started as a dream with a piece of land. Now your custom-designed home has become a reality. It's time to start living in the special place you've created. Enjoy!

Special thanks to Orren Pickell Designers and Builders, Bannockburn, IL, and Centurian Development, Scottsdale, AZ, for their contributions to this article.

continued from page **141**

UNIQUE HOMES OF CHARLOTTE..**(704) 341-3390**
  7621 Little Ave, Suite 201, Charlotte Fax: (704) 341-4984
  See Ad on Page: 142, 143, 144, 145
  <u>Principal/Owner:</u> Bruce L. Bleiman
  <u>Additional Information:</u> My position is to create & build truly outstanding homes
  as "works of art" which display remarkable and unmistakable excellence!!!

HUBERT WHITLOCK BUILDERS, INC. ....**(704) 384-9577**
  5672 International Dr, Suite 212, Charlotte Fax: (704) 364-8579
  See Ad on Page: 177
  <u>Principal/Owner:</u> Steven Whitlock

WOLFE HOMES ....**(336) 299-2969**
  200-J Pomona Dr., Greensboro Fax: (336) 299-2949
  See Ad on Page: 162, 163
  <u>Principal/Owner:</u> Jim Wolfe and David Schenck
  <u>Website:</u> www.wolfehomes.net <u>e-mail:</u> info@wolfehomes.net
  <u>Additional Information:</u> Jim Wolfe and David Schenck are known for creating
  award-winning custom residences that combine comfort, elegance and value.

173

THERE ARE HOMES, AND THEN THERE ARE SOUTHERN STRUCTURES.

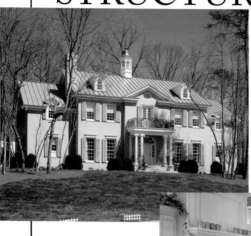

Experience the difference, At Southern Structures, we have a history of providing the homebuyer the quality, custom-built home they desire, with the quality workmanship and attention to detail they deserve. Need proof? We'll put you in contact with our Southern Structures homeowners. Call Martha Faw today - your personal builder with the award winning touch.

SOUTHERN STRUCTURES

CUSTOM HOME DESIGN

NEW CONSTRUCTION & RENOVATION

PFAHL

C U S T O M   B U I L D E R S , I N C

Kevin & Susan Pfahl
1200 The Plaza, Suite E
Charlotte, NC 28205
704-342-1065

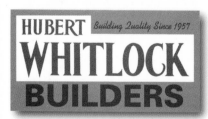

WITH EACH FOUNDATION
LIES SOMETHING MUCH STRONGER
THAN BRICKS AND MORTAR.
A NAME...

GARYJOBE
BUILDER

GARY JOBE BUILDER, INC.
421 North Edgeworth St.
Greensboro, NC 27401
Phone: 336.272.2772

DENNIS SOSEBEE CUSTOM HOMES, INC.

P.O. Box 38723
Greensboro, NC 27438
Phone 336.288.1072
Fax 336.288.6019

"We take great pride in our work, our reputation and our relationship with our clients. We welcome the opportunity to build a custom home for you."

—Dennis Sosebee

=== *Exceptional Homes* ===

Unique design and meticulous detail in every home...

Sunstar
Homes

Remodeling
Specialists

NEW MOON BUILDERS ....**(704) 377-1820**
338 S. Sharen Amity Road, Charlotte   Fax: (704) 367-1747
See Ad on Page: 185
e-mail: newmoonbuilder@cs.com
Additional Information: New Moon Builders specializes in quality residential additions
and renovations as well as custom home building.

SPAIN CONSTRUCTION ....**(704) 554-0041**
1400 Sharon Road West, Suite C13, Charlotte
See Ad on Page: 184
Principal/Owner: Don DellaMea, GC CR

SWIMMER CONSTRUCTION..**(704) 375-7177**
725 Providence Road, Charlotte   Fax: (704) 376-7528
See Ad on Page: 186, 187
Principal/Owner: Scott L. Swimmer
e-mail: swimrsync@aol.com

SPAIN CONSTRUCTION

Remodeling Since 1970

1400 Sharon Road West • Suite C13
Charlotte, NC 28210
704.554.0041

DINA LOWERY'S ───────
─────────STUDIO OF DESIGN

3019 selwyn avenue | charlotte nc 28209
704.529.2680 | 704.529.2686 fax
dinalowery@prodigy.net
by appointment

HERB HIGHSMITH CYNTHIA A. ESTILL

HighsmitH
INTERIORS

106 & 107 Glenwood Avenue
Raleigh, North Carolina 27603 • 919-832-6275

193

Inner Beauty

It may be as simple as a fresh look at the familiar. Or it may be an involved process requiring major renovation. In either case, interior designers can bring your ideas to life by demystifying the daunting task of designing a home. With their years of professional experience and the tools that they have at their fingertips, designers can orchestrate, layer by layer, design elements that compose an inviting and harmonious décor. For this collaboration to be a success, however, requires communication and trust. By listening to your dreams and by understanding your needs, designers can fashion workable rooms that are visual delights, reflecting your personality and your spirit. The end result of a productive partnership should be a happy homeowner who can exclaim, "I've always known that this was a great house, but now it's home!"

Photo courtesy of **F. Taylor Johnson Interiors**
Photo by **Paul G. Beswick**

WHERE STRUCTURE MEETS INSPIRATION

A great interior designer, like a great architect or builder, sees space creatively, applying years of education and experience to deliver a distinguished residence at the highest level of quality in an organized, professional manner. Intensely visual, these talented individuals imprint a home with the spirit and personality of the family living there.

Creativity, that special talent to see the possibilities in a living room, library, or little reading nook, is the most important asset an interior designer will bring to a project. Particularly in upper-end interiors, where the expense of sumptuous furnishings is often a secondary concern, the creative vision is what makes a room extraordinary.

A top quality interior designer who is licensed by the state is well educated in the field of interior design, usually holding a bachelor's or master's degree in the subject. This educational background coupled with practical experience is vital. You need not know where to get the best down-filled pillows or when French fabric mills close each summer. You need not learn the difference between French Country and English Country, how to match patterns, or how to correctly balance a floor plan. Rely on a knowledgeable designer for that information.

A great interior designer also handles the "nuts and bolts" business end of the project. With skill and experience in placing and tracking orders, scheduling shipping, delivery and installation, the designer can bring your project to its perfect conclusion.

AN INTERIOR DESIGNER IS A TEAM MEMBER

Choose an interior designer when you select your architect, builder, and landscape architect. A skilled designer can collaborate with the architect on matters such as window and door location, appropriate room size, and practical and accent lighting plans. In new construction and remodeling, try to make your floor plan and furniture choices simultaneously, to avoid common design problems, such as traffic corridors running through a formal space or awkward locations of electrical outlets.

CREATE THE BEST CLIENT-DESIGNER RELATIONSHIP

Talk to the best interior designers in the area and they'll tell you how exciting and gratifying it is for them when a client is involved in the process. This is happening as more homeowners turn their attention to hearth and home, dedicating their time and resources to achieve a style they love.

FIVE THINGS YOU SHOULD KNOW

1. Know what level of guidance you want: a person to handle every detail, someone to collaborate with you or simply an occasional consultation.
2. Know what you're trying to achieve. Start an Idea Notebook, filling it with pictures of rooms you like and don't like. This will help you define your style and stay true to your goal.
3. Know your budget. Prices of high-end furnishings know no upper limit. Adopt a "master plan" to phase in design elements if your tastes are outpacing your pocketbook.
4. Know what's going on. Always ask; don't assume. Design is not a mystical process.
5. Know yourself. Don't get blinded by beauty. Stay focused on what makes you feel "at home," and you'll be successful.

To establish the most successful and pleasant relationship with an interior designer, make a personal commitment to be involved.

Start by defining your needs, in terms of service and the end result. Have an interior designer involved during the architectural drawing phase of a new or renovation project, and get the process started early. Be clear about how much help you want from a designer. Some homeowners have a strong sense of what they want and simply need a consultant-type relationship. Others want significant guidance from a professional who will oversee the entire process.

Set up a relationship that encourages an open exchange of ideas. In pursuit of personal style, you need to trust a professional designer to interpret your thoughts and needs. You must be comfortable saying, "No, I don't like that," and receptive to hearing, "I don't think that's a good idea."

Be forthcoming about your budget. Not all interiors are guided by a budget, but the majority are. Your designer must know and respect your financial parameters and priorities. If a gorgeous dining room table is a top priority, objets d'art can be added later as you find them. Prices of exquisite furniture, custom-carved cabinets, and other high-end furnishings know no upper limit. Be realistic about what you will spend and what you expect to achieve. Do some research in furniture stores and specialty shops, starting with those showcased in this book. If your expectations temporarily exceed your budget, phase in the décor over a period of time.

Be inquisitive as the design unfolds. This is a creative effort on your behalf, so let yourself enjoy it, understand it and be stimulated by it.

START THINKING VISUALLY: STOP, LOOK AND CLIP

Before you start scheduling initial interviews with interior designers, start compiling an Idea Notebook – it's the best tool for developing an awareness of your personal style. Spend a weekend or two with a pair of scissors, a notebook, and a stack of magazines, (or add a section to the Idea Notebook you made to inspire your architecture and building plans). Make this a record of your personal style. Include pictures of your favorite rooms, noting colors, fabrics, tile, carpet, fixtures, the way light filters through a curtain, anything that strikes your fancy. On those pictures, circle the design elements that you'd like to incorporate into your own home décor and make comments regarding those elements you don't care for. Think hard about what you love and loathe in your current residence. Start to look at the entire environment as a rich source of design

UNDERSTANDING "ECLECTIC"

Eclectic means "not following any one system, but selecting and using what seems best from all systems."

Its popularity in interior design stems from the unique look it creates. Mixing the best from different styles creates a dynamic look that's totally different from an application of one chosen style. The overall effect is casual and comfortable, "dressed up" in a less formal way.

Eclectic can mean a mixing of styles within one room, like a rich Oriental rug paired with a denim sofa, or between rooms, like an 18th century dining room leading into an Early American kitchen. The possibilities for accents and appointments are unlimited because there are no restrictions.

One Person's Project Estimate:

Time To Redesign

It's fun to imagine, but what might it actually cost to undertake a project described in this chapter? The example below describes a typical project and gives a general estimate of the costs involved.

Project Description
Redesigning a 15 x 22 sq. ft. living room in a mid-scale price range.

Initial consultation $500
During the initial consultation, dimensions of the room are measured and photos taken of the room's distinctive qualities (unusual architecture, fireplaces, French doors, etc.). Next, a floor plan is done with recommendations of furniture placement.

Cost per hour (5 hour minimum) $100/hr
These charges apply to trips to local showrooms, the design center or antique shops to choose fabrics, furniture, and accessories. After the furniture is ordered, attention is turned to window treatments (photographing the windows and using the pictures as sketchboards to design various treatments, fabrics and colors). When designing kitchens and bathrooms, time may also be spent with clients and contractors discussing styles of cabinetry, countertops and flooring.

New rug (oriental or custom) $8,000

Furniture: Transitional (contemporary upholstery, traditional wood pieces)
     Sofa $3,000
     Chairs (2) .... $1,000 ea.
     Coffee table $2,000
     End tables (2) .... $1,000 ea.
     Sofa table $2,000
     French Be'rgre chair $3,000

Lamps (1 bronze, 2 porcelain) $1,200
Lighted wall sconces $1,000
Artwork $2,000
     1 large piece over sofa
     1 smaller piece over the fireplace
New paint
     Labor and paint (one color) $1,500
Accessories $3,000
     Silver tray with crystal decanter and 2 brandy snifters, large candlesticks.
     Crystal vase and several unusual picture frames in sterling and brass.

TOTAL $31,700

Note: The entire cost for a room design does not necessarily have to be paid at one time. Many designers are willing to work with a client over several years, adding a few items at a time, in order to create the look that is right for the client and his/her surroundings.

Lighted wall sconces
to flank the fireplace

Contemporary
chair

ideas. Movies, billboards, architecture, clothing – all are fascinating sources for visual stimulation.

Then, when you hold that initial meeting, you, too, will have a book of ideas to share. Although a smart designer will be able to coax this information from you, it's tremendously more reliable to have visual representations than to depend on a verbal description. It also saves a tremendous amount of time.

THE INTERIOR DESIGN PROCESS: GETTING TO KNOW YOU

Give yourself time to interview at least two interior designers. Invite them to your home for a tour of your current residence and a look at items you wish to use in the new environment. If you're building or remodeling, an interior designer can be helpful with your overall plans when he or she is given the opportunity to get involved early in the building process.

During the initial meeting, count on your intuition to guide you toward the best designer for you. Decorating a home is an intimate and very personal experience, so a comfortable relationship with a high degree of trust is absolutely necessary for a good result. You may adore what a designer did for a friend, but if you can't easily express your ideas, or if you feel he or she isn't interested in your point of view, don't pursue the relationship. Unless you can imagine yourself working with a designer two or three homes from now, keep interviewing.

You may wish to hire a designer for one room before making a commitment to do the whole house.

Some designers maintain a high degree of confidentiality regarding their clients, but if possible, get references and contact them, especially clients with whom they've worked on more than one home. Be sure to ask about the quality of follow-up service.

Be prepared to talk in specific terms about your project, and to honestly assess your lifestyle. For a home or a room to work well, function must be considered along with the evolving style. Designers ask many questions; some of them may be:

• What function should each room serve? Will a living room double as a study? Will a guest room also be an exercise area?

• Who uses the rooms? Growing children, adults, business associates? Which are shared and which are private?

• What safety and maintenance issues must be addressed? A growing family or a family pet may dictate the degree of elegance of a home.

IMMERSE YOURSELF

The more exposure you have to good design, the easier it becomes to develop your own style.

• Haunt the bookstores that have large selections of shelter magazines and stacks of books on decorating, design and architecture.
• Attend show houses, especially the Designer Showcase homes presented twice annually by ASID, and visit model homes, apartments or lofts.

EMBRACE THE MASTER PLAN

Gone are the days when North Carolina homeowners felt the need to move into a "finished" interior. They take their time now, letting the flow of their evolving lifestyle and needs guide them along the way.

- What kind of relationship do you want to establish between the interior and the landscape?

- Style: Formal, casual or a bit of both?

- Are you comfortable with color?

- Are you sentimental, practical?

- Are you naturally organized or disorganized?

- What kind of art do you like? Do you own art that needs to be highlighted or displayed in a certain way? Do you need space for a growing collection?

- Do you feel at home in a dog-eared, low maintenance family room or do you soothe your soul in an opulent leather chair, surrounded by rich cabinetry and Oriental rugs?

- What kind of furniture do you like? Queen Anne, contemporary, American Arts and Crafts, casual wicker, or eclectic mixing of styles?

- What words describe the feeling you want to achieve? Cheerful, cozy, tranquil, elegant, classic?

COMPUTING THE INTERIOR DESIGN FEE

Designers use individual contracts, standard contracts drawn up by the American Society of Interior Designers (ASID), or letters of agreements as legal documents. The ASID contract outlines seven project phases – programming, schematic, design development, contract documents, contract administration, project representation beyond basic services, and additional services. It outlines the designer's special responsibilities, the owner's responsibilities, the fees agreed upon, and the method of payments to the designer, including reimbursement of expenses.

Payment deadlines vary. Payments may be due at the completion of each project phase, on a monthly or quarterly basis, or as orders are made. You can usually expect to pay a retainer or a 50 percent deposit on goods as they are ordered, 40 percent upon the start of installation, and the balance when the job is completed.

Design fees, which may be based on "current market rate," are also computed in various ways. They may be charged on a flat fee or hourly basis, or may be tied to retail costs. Expect fees of approximately $100 an hour, varying by experience, reputation and workload. If an hourly rate is being used, ask if there is a cap per day, and if different rates are charged for an assistants or drafter's time. Percentages may be figured as a certain amount above the retail or trade price, and can range from 15 to 100 percent. Make sure you understand your fee

PROFESSIONAL DESIGNATIONS
ASID (American Society of Interior Designers)/Carolinas Chapter
PO Box 33697
Charlotte, NC 28233
919-569-2130
www.asid.org

IIDA (International Interior Design Association)
International Headquarters
998 Merchandise Mart
Chicago, IL 60654
312.467.1950
www.iida.org
email:
IIDAhq@iida.org
Offers referrals to North Carolina homeowners.

Designers who add ASID or IIDA after their names are certified members of the organization.

199

CAN YOU WEAR WHITE AFTER LABOR DAY?

There are colors and emotions for every season. Let your designer know if you want to be able to change the look and feel of your home to reflect the seasons.

MAKE LIGHTING A PRIORITY

The trend toward a comprehensive lighting programs as part of good interior design is catching on in North Carolina luxury homes. Appropriate light and well-designed accent lighting are very important to the overall comfort and functionality of a home. Neither the stunning volume ceiling nor the cozy breakfast nook can reach their potential if the lighting is wrong. Ask your interior designer for his or her lighting ideas. These choices need to be made in coordination with the building timeline, so plan and place orders early.

structure early on. Separate design fees may be charged by the hour, room, or entire project. It is imperative to trust your designer and rely on his or her reputation of delivering a top quality project in an honest, reliable fashion. You must feel you're being given a valuable service for a fair price.

If you work with a designer at a retail store, a design service fee ranging from $100 to $500 may be charged and applied against purchases.

FROM THE MIND'S EYE TO REALITY

Once you've found a designer who you like and trust, and have signed a clear, specific agreement, you're ready to embark on the adventure.

A good designer knows his or her way around the masses of products and possibilities. Such a person will guide you through upscale retail outlets and to craftspeople known only to a fortunate few in the trade. You can be a "kid in a candy store."

Just as you've allowed time to carefully consider and reconsider architectural blueprints, temper your enthusiasm to rush into decisions regarding your interiors. Leave fabric swatches where you see them day after day. Look at paint samples in daylight, evening light and artificial light. If possible, have everyone in the family "test sit" a kitchen chair for a week before ordering the whole set, and play with furniture placement. This small investment of time will pay handsomely in the end.

Be prepared to wait for your interiors to be installed. It's realistic to allow eight months to complete a room, and eight to 12 months to decorate an entire home.

Decide if you want your interiors to be installed piecemeal or all at once. Many designers recommend waiting for one installation, if you have the patience. Homeowners tend to rethink their original decisions when pieces are brought in as they arrive. By waiting for one installation, they treat themselves to a stunning visual and emotional thrill. ■

Creating a **Beautiful** Interior

You have found your paradise. You have fallen in love with the area around your new home. The views are spectacular. The entrance is grand and suitably impressive. The great room will be a place where family, friends and visitors will all feel at ease, and all will be welcomed within. You can envision it, but how do you get from dreaming the dream to living it? Beautiful rooms do not just happen. They are the result of careful planning by the homeowner and an interior designer. While you may have an idea of what you would like, or have a desire for a particular effect, it is the interior designer who can take your dream and turn it into something magnificent.

We have taken one family's dream, to create a spectacular, yet comforting home, and followed that project from the day the client bought the home to the day the rooms they once dreamed of became rooms they now live in.

The following timeline is designed to give you an idea of how long it may take to complete an interior design project of this magnitude, and what the steps will be along the way. While the steps will most likely remain the same, the timeline may shorten or lengthen depending on your individual project. We have also included a few helpful tips and ideas, to further ensure that your project can go as smoothly as possible.

Project
Description

T he project included redesigning every existing room along with planning and decorating a 3,500 sq. ft. addition. In all, the home has two family rooms, a great room, a theater, kitchen and dining rooms, screen porches with dining, and six bedrooms and baths. There is also a two-bedroom, two-bath guest house on the property. The project took approximately 18 months, which is a long time for a design-only project, but not long for new construction.

In
Conclusion

N ow that you have seen an interior design project guided from beginning to end, it's time to embark on your own project. Yes, it will take some time to complete. And it will require a certain amount of involvement from you and communication with the designer. But in the end, you will have a space that is uniquely yours. You will have rooms that welcome you in, views you enjoy, furnishings that fit and details that express who you are. It can be a long journey, but one with a remarkable payoff.

Thanks to Janet Mesic Mackie for her contribution of photography for this timeline.

HERB HIGHSMITH INTERIORS ....**(919) 829-5999**
  106/107 Glenwood Ave., Raleigh   Fax: (919) 831-0434
  See Ad on Page: 192
  <u>Principal/Owner:</u> Herb Highsmith

KRM DESIGN ....**(704) 373-0275**
  1412 E. Fourth Street Suite B, Charlotte   Fax: (704) 342-2316
  See Ad on Page: 213
  <u>Principal/Owner:</u> Mercedes I. Burum

DINA LOWERY'S STUDIO OF DESIGN ....**(704) 529-2680**
  3019 Selwyn Avenue, Charlotte   Fax: (704) 529-2686
  See Ad on Page: 190, 191, 432
  <u>Principal/Owner:</u> Dina Lowery
  <u>e-mail:</u> dinalowery@prodigy.net

CAROLE F. SMYTH ANTIQUES & INTERIORS ....**(704) 553-2653**
  4607 Curraghmore Road, Charlotte   Fax: (704) 553-2169
  See Ad on Page: 212
  <u>Principal/Owner:</u> Carole F. Smyth, ASID, IIDA
  <u>Website:</u> www.antiqnet.com <u>e-mail:</u> e-smyth@mindspring.com
  <u>Additional Information:</u> A 32 year old design firm specializing in custom interiors
  and fine antiques for clients who want excitement and quality.

LEO DOWELL INTERIORS ....**(704) 334-3817**
  501 E. Morehead Street, Suite 2, Charlotte   Fax: (704) 334-5830
  See Ad on Page: 214, 215
  <u>Principal/Owner:</u> Leo Dowell
  <u>Website:</u> www.leodowellinteriors.com <u>e-mail:</u> leodowellinteriors@att.net
  <u>Additional Information:</u> Conceptual designs for residential custom homes from
  the ground up through the last intention detail.

DONALD DRAGGOO INTERIORS ....**(336) 273-9418**
  525 State St., Greensboro   Fax: (336) 273-2838
  See Ad on Page: 224, 225
  <u>Principal/Owner:</u> Donald Draggoo
  <u>e-mail:</u> Draggoo@bellsouth.net
  <u>Additional Information:</u> Residential and Commercial Architectural and Interior Design.

ELEGANT INTERIORS ....**(336) 856-0003**
  2100 Fairfax Rd., Suite 101-D, Greensboro   Fax: (336) 315-5509
  See Ad on Page: 223
  <u>Principal/Owner:</u> Elizabeth Breach
  <u>Website:</u> elegantinteriors.ebroach.net <u>e-mail:</u> elegntint@aol.com

F. TAYLOR JOHNSON INTERIOR DESIGN ....**(704) 525-7440**
  3332 Selwyn Avenue, Charlotte   Fax: (704) 525-7440
  See Ad on Page: 226
  <u>Principal/Owner:</u> F. Taylor Johnson
  <u>e-mail:</u> tjoh3332@aol.com

209

continued on page **222**

A full-service 32 year old firm specializing in custom interiors and fine antiques for clients who want exciting, quality design.

KRM
DESIGN
LTD

Interior Design
Elegant Furnishings
& Accessories

KRM Design Showroom
1412 East Fourth Street
Suite B
Charlotte, NC 28204

Contact:
Kathy McElroy, Allied ASID
704-373-0275

European Homes

Style Custom Homes and Interiors

Exquisitely Unorthodox

216

DINA LOWERY'S STUDIO OF DESIGN

Dina Lowery:
"This 1970s home was filled with unmistakable decorating trends from the period - Williamsburg blue walls, medium-stained wainscoting, gray carpeting and a standard masonry fireplace. A remarkable transformation began when the trim and walls were painted in warm golden hues. New lighting was installed to promote ambiance and high-light the artwork. The fireplace wall, once brick, became an architectural detail that is now a piece of artwork in itself. The warmth of color and interest of texture makes the room livable and inviting to lure the family or guests in to enjoy a game of chess or backgammon."

Desi

PAMELA D. LEE INTERIOR DESIGN

Pamela D. Lee:

"To maximize the limited space in this drawing and music room, accessories are kept to a minimum and arranged in a collective composition. The vivid color on the walls makes for a perfect backdrop against the neutral upholstery and richly ornamented antique side chairs. Strong accents of orange and other clear colors, as well as contrasting textures - such as the use of bold burlap against the window softened by an overlay of sheer fabric - add interest and a 'touch of Tuscany.' The infusion of these elements creates a sense of warmth, comfort and subtle elegance."

Photo by **Donna Bise**

ners

LEO DOWELL INTERIORS

Leo Dowell:

"My design philosophy of 'dusting of centuries' came to life in this home, creating a brand new interior that looked comfortable and well lived-in. The furniture was purchased before the home was built, so we designed niches on either side of the fireplace, lined with stone from the home's exterior, to highlight two chests. The Mexican pinon stone fireplace was also lined with 'stone' made of concrete, then aged by hand with charcoal to simulate decades of use. The final tongue-in-cheek effect is the trompe l'oeil in the corner painted to appear the ceiling has been opened for repairs."

Photo by **Joseph Lapeyra**

Desi

219

F. TAYLOR JOHNSON INTERIOR DESIGN

F. Taylor Johnson:

"Designing a room for relaxation and study in a long narrow space is a challenge of proportion. Everything used in the room must be scaled properly. We used a long narrow sofa and small club chairs to allow for comfort and relaxation. The rich colors in the Oriental carpet, draperies and upholstery gave us the atmosphere of quiet permanence and security. This is a wonderful place to retire at the end of the day."

ners

GAYE MITCHUM INTERIORS

Gaye Mitchum:
"This gathering place was designed to accommodate the everyday lifestyle of a busy family. The project was an eclectic mix of hues, materials, textures and styles. Cashmere-finish cabinets are detailed with high column pilasters and intricate carved corbels. Specialty features, like a wine cooler, pot-filler faucet, hand-blown glass light fixtures, and a mosaic glass backsplash, give the room an updated, but classic style."

Desig

CAROLE F. SMYTH INTERIORS

Carole F. Smyth, ASID:

"A small 9 ft. by 17 ft. space was outfitted as a guest room using a textured, light wallcovering and a custom-woven floorcovering, to give the room a tailored feeling. A twin daybed is placed against the far wall to save floor space. Chairs and a wood table are dramatic, but small in size, to also create the feeling of space. Windows are treated simply, to let in light, and all clutter is eliminated."

Photo by Leslie Wright Dow

221

Interior Designers

continued from page **209**

PAMELA D. LEE INTERIOR DESIGN, INC....**(704) 373-1590**
601 South Cedar Street, Suite 126, Charlotte   Fax: (704) 373-1592
See Ad on Page: 210, 211
Principal/Owner: Pamela D. Lee
e-mail: pamdlee@aol.com
Additional Information: Award winning, full service design studio offering custom
window treatments and furniture, interior finishes, accessories, etc. Members of
the Interior Design Society and ASID.

GAYE MITCHUM INTERIORS...**(704) 334-9488**
2108 South Blvd., Suite 104, Charlotte   Fax: (704) 377-4036
See Ad on Page: 227
Principal/Owner: Gaye Mitchum
Website: www.gayemitchum.com

G. ALLEN SCRUGGS, ASID...**(336) 788-5188**
2416 Union Cross Rd., Winston-Salem   Fax: (336) 650-0383
See Ad on Page: 228
e-mail: nekomo@triad.rr.com

Elegant Interiors

An Elegant Approach To Decorating

COMPLETE DECORATING SERVICES FOR COMMERCIAL AND RESIDENTIAL LOCATIONS

Elizabeth Broach
336-856-0003

2100 Fairfax Rd
Suite 101-D
Greensboro, NC 27407

Donald Draggoo Interiors

DONALD W. DRAGGOO

525 STATE STREET ● GREENSBORO, NORTH CAROLINA 27405
336 . 273 . 9418 ● FAX 336 . 273 . 2838
524 SOUTH ELM STREET ● GREENSBORO, NORTH CAROLINA 27406
336 . 273 . 9415 ● FAX 336 . 273 . 9455

F. TAYLOR JOHNSON
INTERIOR DESIGN

3332 Selwyn Ave. Charlotte, NC 28209
704 525 7440 • tjoh3332@aol.com

GAYE MITCHUM INTERIORS

Kingswood Homes, Photo by Pat Shanklin

IDS, ALLIED MEMBER ASID, CQRID #400136

2108 SOUTH BOULEVARD, SUITE 104
CHARLOTTE, NORTH CAROLINA 28203
(704) 334-9488 • FAX(704) 377-4036
WWW.GAYEMITCHUM.COM

g. allen scruggs, a.s.i.d.
j. douglas myers
336 788-5188
nekomo@triad.rr.com

Interior design that reflects...style, quality, and depth of experience

Work published in:

Architectural Digest   *Southern Living*   *House Beautiful*

Finally...
North Carolina's Own
Home & Design
Sourcebook

The **North Carolina Home Book** is your final destination when searching for home remodeling, building and decorating resources. This comprehensive, hands-on sourcebook to building, remodeling, decorating, furnishing, and landscaping a luxury home is required reading for the serious and discriminating homeowner. With more than 500 full-color, beautiful pages, the **North Carolina Home Book** is the most complete and well-organized reference to the home industry. This hardcover volume covers all aspects of the process, includes listings of hundreds of industry professionals, and is accompanied by informative and valuable editorial discussing the most recent trends. Ordering your copy of the **North Carolina Home Book** now can ensure that you have the blueprints to your dream home,

in your hand, today.

Order your copy now!

NORTH CAROLINA
HOME
BOOK

Published by
The Ashley Group
8420 University Executive
Suite 810
Charlotte, NC 28262
704.549.3687 fax: 704.549.3695
E-mail: ashleybooksales@cahners.com

The Ashley Group Luxury Home Resource Collection

The **Ashley Group (www.theashleygroup.com)** is pleased to offer as your final destination when searching for home improvement and luxury resources the following **Home Books** in your local market. Available Now: *Chicago, Washington D.C., South Florida, Los Angeles, Dallas/Fort Worth, Detroit, Colorado, New York, Atlanta, Arizona, Philadelphia, San Diego, North Carolina,* and *Las Vegas.* These comprehensive, hands-on guides to building, remodeling, decorating, furnishing, and landscaping a luxury home, are required reading for the serious and selective homeowner. With over 700 full-color, beautiful pages, the **Home Book** series in each market covers all aspects of the building and remodeling process, including listings of hundreds of local industry professionals, accompanied by informative and valuable editorial discussing the most recent trends.

Order your copies today and make your dream come true!

CAN BECOME
A REALITY...

235

Natural
Selection

Landscaping is the only design area that is by nature intended to evolve over time. The philosophy behind landscape design has evolved as well. From traditional European formality to the naturalism of Prairie Style, to the simplicity and order of Far Eastern influences, your landscape should be as unique a design statement as your home itself.

More and more people are blurring the divisions between inside and outside environments, with expanses of windows, patios designed to act as "outdoor rooms" and various types of glass and screened enclosures to enjoy the outdoors whatever the weather. Landscape becomes almost an architectural element at times, creating an interplay and synthesis of indoors and outdoors.

Water gardens are growing in popularity as people learn that they are ecosystems in their own right, requiring little additional time or attention once they are established. Think of it: the soothing splash of a waterfall or babbling brook right in your own backyard!

Photo courtesy of **TG&R Landscape Group**

VIEWS AND VISTAS

First you choose your views, then you build your home. To create a harmonious balance between your home and its surroundings, your architect should be invited to visit the site of your new home, and to meet with your landscape architect. The site can often serve as a catalyst, inspiring a design that responds to the uniqueness of the site. When all the team members are included, important details (like the location of your air conditioning units) can be discussed and settled, making for the best results for you and your family.

OUTDOOR DÉCOR

As North Carolina homeowners get more involved in their yards and gardens, they learn to "see" outdoor rooms and take deep pleasure in decorating them. Arbors, sculpture, tables, benches, water features, or any piece of whimsy add delightful decorating. Hedges or fences create natural partitions. The results are appealing, comfortable and richly rewarding.

GETTING BACK TO THE GARDEN

Think of the land as a canvas for a work of environmental art. Think of the landscape professional as an artist who uses nature to translate your needs and desires into a living, breathing reality. A formal English garden or seemingly artless arrangements of native plantings, a winding cobblestone walkway leading from a hand-laid brick driveway — these are the kinds of possibilities you can explore. When you work with a professional who is personally committed to superior work and service, designing a landscape is full of creativity, new ideas and satisfying results.

GETTING A LANDSCAPE STARTED

Selecting a landscape professional to create and maintain a distinctive landscape is one of the most important decisions you'll make as a homeowner. In making your decision, consider these questions:

• Are you landscaping a new construction home? There are critical decisions to be made early in the home building planning process that concern the landscape. Interview and work with professionals who have considerable experience in doing excellent work with new construction projects. Make them part of your team and have them meet with your architect, interior designer and builder early in the project.

• Do you want to hire a landscape architect or a landscape designer? Landscape architects have met the criteria to be registered by the state. Many hold university degrees in landscape architecture. A landscape designer generally has had training and/or experience in horticulture and landscaping and may also have a background in art.

• Do you want full service? If you want to work with one source, from design through installation to maintenance, only consider those who offer comprehensive service.

Allow time to interview at least two professionals before making a decision. Start early, especially if you plan to install a swimming pool, which should be dug the same time as the foundation of a new home.

Invite the professional to your home to acquaint him or her with your tastes and personality through observing your choices in interior design as well as the current landscape. Have a plat of survey available. Be prepared to answer questions like:

• Do you prefer a formal or informal feel? The formality of symmetrical plantings or the informal look of a natural area?

• Is there a place or feeling you'd like to recreate? Somewhere where you've vacationed, or the place where you grew up?

• What colors do you like? This will impact the flowers chosen for your gardens.

• Are you a gardener? Would you like to be? If you're fond of flower, herb or vegetable gardening, your landscape professional will build the appropriate gardens.

• How will you use the space? Will children use the backyard for recreation? Will you entertain outdoors? If so, will it be during the day or at night? Do you envision a pool, spa, gazebo or tennis court?

• Are you fond of lawn statuary, fountains or other ornamental embellishments?

• What architectural features must be considered? A wrap-around porch, large picture windows? Brick or stone exteriors?

• To what extent will you be involved in the process? Most landscape architects and designers are happy to encourage your involvement in this labor of love. There is a great deal of pleasure to be derived from expressing your personality through the land. A lifelong hobby can take root from this experience. Landscapers say their clients often join garden clubs after the completion of their project, and that many of their rehabbing projects are done for clients who are already avid gardeners.

Landscape professionals expect that you will want to see a portfolio, inquire about their styles, and their experience. You may wish to request permission to visit sites of their installed landscapes. If you have special concerns, such as environmental issues, ask if the landscape professional has any experience in such areas.

COMPUTING LANDSCAPE FEES

It's important to create a workable budget. It's easy to be caught off guard when you get a landscape proposal – it is a significant investment.

To make sure you give the outside of your home the appropriate priority status, plan to invest 10 to 25 percent of the cost of a new home and property in the landscaping. Although landscape elements can be phased in year after year, expect that the majority of the cost will be incurred in the first year. Maintenance costs must also be considered.

Billing practices vary among professionals and depend on the extent of the services you desire. Some charge a flat design fee up front, some charge a one-time fee for a contract that includes everything, some charge a design fee which is

THE LANDSCAPE BUDGET

Basic:
10% of the cost of your home & property
In-depth:
The 10 to 25% rule of thumb applies to your landscapes too. Starting at $90,000:
• Finish grading
• Sodded lawns
• Foundation plantings (all around the house) including some smaller trees
• Walkways of pavers or stone
City Dwellers!
• Soft atmospheric lighting up to the front door and in the back yard
• Asphalt driveway
• Concrete unit pavers or stone patio, or deck
• Perimeter plantings of trees and shrubs for privacy and finished look

A PARTY OF GARDENS

As gardening attracts more devotees in North Carolina, people are rediscovering the satisfaction of creating imaginative gardens. Some ideas: one-color gardens, fragrance gardens, native plant gardens, Japanese gardens.

237

One Person's Project Estimate:

The Price of Being Green

It's fun to imagine, but what might it actually cost to undertake a project described in this chapter? The example below describes a typical project and gives a general estimate of the costs involved.

PROJECT DESCRIPTION

Landscape development of a typical property consisting of new paver patio and walk, retaining wall and approximately 600 sq. ft. of new planting beds along front foundation.

Initial consultation 0

Design contract fees..$500

Hardscape construction
Cut Lanonstone retaining wall (85 face sq. ft.) $4,130
Concrete paver patio and walkway (480 sq. ft.) $7,785

Planting development
Bed preparation (600 sq. ft.) $9,000
Includes: Assorted foundation shrubs
    Four mid-size shade trees
    Assorted perennials
    Annual beds
    New sod for lawn areas

Landscape management..$3,648
One season (April – November) of maintenance of about one-half acre site.
Includes: Weekly mowing and trimming of maintained turf areas
    Monthly pavement edging of sidewalks, patios and driveway
    Weekly landscape debris clean-up of maintained areas
    Monthly cultivation of open bed areas
    Manual weeding
    Preventative weed control
    Granular fertilization of maintained bed areas
    Spade edging of beds
    Selective pruning of oriental trees (less than 12 feet high), shrubs and hedges
    Weekly perennial dead heading of faded flowers
    Groundcover maintenance and pruning
    Spring and Fall clean-up of maintained areas
    Weekly off-site disposal of landscape waste and grass clippings
    Turf fertilization program
    Broadleaf weed control in late Spring and late Summer

TOTAL: **$25,063**

Assorted annuals, perennials and shrubs

Cut Lanonstone retaining wall

Herringbone pattern for concrete patio pavers

LIGHTING YOUR LOT

"Less is more" is the best philosophy when designing an outdoor lighting system. Today's beautiful, functional fixtures are themselves worthy of admiration, but their purpose is to highlight the beauty of your home while providing safe access to your property. Well-established lighting companies and specialty companies offer extensive landscape lighting product lines.

DREAM POOLS

Yours for $60,000: Custom-designed mid-sized pool with a deep end, spa, custom lighting, cleaning system, remote control functions, cover, deck. Yours for $200,000: A custom-designed Roman-style pool with bar stools, a small wading pool, elevated spa and elaborate waterfall. Specialized lighting, built-in planters, automated hydraulic cover, top-of-the-line automated cleaning system, all with remote control functions.

waived if you select them to complete the project, and some build a design fee into the installation and/or maintenance cost.

A PROFESSIONAL DEVELOPS AN ENVIRONMENT

While you're busy imagining glorious gardens, your landscaper will be assessing practical issues like grading and drainage, the location of sewers, utility lines and existing trees, where and when the sun hits the land, and the quality of the soil.

This important first step, the site analysis, should take place before construction has even begun, in the case of a new house. Site work helps ensure that the blueprints for your house won't make your landscape dreams impossible to achieve, and vice versa. If you've told your builder you want a breakfast nook, you'll probably get one regardless of the fact that it requires taking out a tree you value.

If you're considering installing a custom driveway or sidewalk, this early stage is the time to inform your builder. Ask your builder not to do construction outside the building envelope. You and your landscape professionals will design and build your driveway and walkways.

Expect the design process to take at least six weeks. During this time, the designer is developing a plan for the hardscape, which includes all of the man-made elements of your outdoor environment, and the many layers of softscape, which are the actual plantings. You can expect to be presented with a plan view that is workable and in harmony with your home, as well as your budget.

Hardscape elements, like irrigation systems and pavements, will be installed first, before a new house is completely finished. Softscape will go in later.

During this landscape project, you most likely have begun to appreciate the special nature of landscape and will not be surprised if your completed project does not look "complete." A landscape should be given time in the hands of nature to come to maturity: three years for perennials, five years for shrubs, and 15 years for trees.

LUXURY LIVING WITH A CUSTOM-DESIGNED POOL

The beauty and value of a custom-designed swimming pool are unmatched. A welcome design element to the landscape, a pool adds to the overall property value of the residence, and creates greater use and enjoyment of the yard. As area families spend more and more of their leisure time at home, a pool answers their dreams of living well at home.

Deciding to build a swimming pool is best done as a new home is being designed so the pool can enhance the home and landscape architecture. By integrating the pool into the overall scheme, you'll be able to establish a realistic budget. One of the biggest mistakes homeowners make when purchasing a pool is not initially getting all the features they want. It's difficult and costly to add features later.

The design process is time-consuming. You may have four or more meetings with your pool professional before finalizing the design. Pool projects can be started at almost any time of year, so avoid getting caught in the busy season, spring to summer. Start getting approvals in January if you want to be enjoying your pool in the summer. The building process takes about two months, after obtaining permits. You should plan to have your pool dug at the same time as the home foundation. Pool construction is integrated with surrounding decking, so make sure your landscape architect, pool builder, or hardscape contractor is coordinating the effort.

OUTDOOR LIVING

Today's homeowners, having invested the time and resources to create a spectacular environment, are ready to "have it all" in their own backyards.

Decks, gazebos, and increasingly, screened rooms, are popular features of today's upscale homes. The extended living space perfectly suits our "cocooning" lifestyle, offering more alternatives for entertaining, relaxation, and family time at home. Many new homes tout outdoor living space as a most tantalizing feature.

Decks and outdoor rooms offer extra living space and are functional enough to host almost any occasion. With thoughtful and proper design, they fulfill our dreams of an outdoor getaway spot. Decks and terraces offer extra living space and are functional enough to host almost any occasion. With thoughtful and proper design, it fulfills our dreams of an outdoor getaway spot. A multi-level deck built up and around mature trees can feel like a treehouse. A spa built into a cedar deck, hidden under a trellis, can make you believe you're in a far-off paradise.

With so many options available, building a new deck provides a unique opportunity for homeowners to give their creativity free rein.

EVERY KID'S FANTASY

In a yard with plenty of flat area: a wood construction expandable play system with several slides, including a spiral slide, crawl tunnels and bridges to connect fort and structures, a tic-tac-toe play panel, three swings, climbing ropes, fire pole, gymnastics equipment (trapeze, turning bar), sandbox pit, and a built-in picnic table with benches. Price Tag: around $12,000

In a smaller yard: a wood construction expandable play system with a small fort, two swings and a single slide. Price Tag: around $1,400

241

THE FINAL EVALUATION

When the landscape is installed, conduct a final, on-site evaluation. You should evaluate the finished design, find out what elements will be installed later and learn more about how the plan will evolve over time. You, the landscape designer or architect, and project manager should be involved.

Landscaping

THINKING ABOUT OUTDOOR LIVING

A n on-site meeting with a licensed contractor who is an expert in landscape building or a landscape architect is the first step in designing and building a deck, patio, or any outdoor structure. An experienced professional will guide you through the conceptualization by asking questions like these:

- Why are you building the structure? For business entertaining, family gatherings, child or teen parties, private time?

- Do you envision a secluded covered area, a wide open expanse, or both?

- Do you want a single level, or two or more levels (the best option for simultaneous activities)?

- Will it tie in with current or future plans?

- How do you want to landscape the perimeter?

- Do you want benches, railings, trellises, or other stylish options, like built-in counters with gas grills, or recessed lighting under benches or railings?

Don't let obstacles block your thinking. Your gas grill can be moved. Decks are often built around trees and can convert steep slopes into usable space.

Once a design has been settled upon, expect three to four weeks to pass before a deck or gazebo is completed. In the busy spring and summer months, it most likely will take longer. The time required to get a building permit (usually two to four weeks) must also be considered.

If you're landscaping during this time, be sure to coordinate the two projects well in advance. Building can wreak havoc on new plantings and your lawn will be stressed during construction.

DISTINCTIVE OUTDOOR SURFACES

D riveways, walkways, patios, decks and wood terraces, and hardscape features were once relegated to "last minute" status, with a budget to match. Today they are being given the full and careful attention they deserve. A brick paver driveway can be made to blend beautifully with the color of the brick used on the house. Natural brick stairways and stoops laid by master crafters add distinctive detail and value. Custom-cut curved bluestone steps, hand selected by an experienced paving contractor, provide years of pride and pleasure.

Hardscape installation doesn't begin until your new home is nearly complete, but for your own budgeting purposes, have decisions made no later than home mid-construction phase.

A TYPICAL LANDSCAPE DESIGN TIMETABLE

- **One to two weeks to get the project on the boards**

  +

- **One to two weeks to do the actual site and design work and prepare plans**

  +

- **One week to coordinate calendars and schedule presentation meeting**

  +

- **One to two weeks to leave the plans with the client and get their feedback**

  +

- **One week to incorporate changes, create and get approval on a final design**

  =

  FIVE TO EIGHT WEEKS

THE TIGHT SQUEEZE

When homes get bigger, backyards get smaller. A landscape architect will be attentive to keeping all aspects of your plan in proper balance.

To interview a paving or hardscape contractor, set up an on-site meeting so you can discuss the nature of the project and express your ideas. Be ready to answer questions like:

• Will the driveway be used by two or three cars, or more? Do you need it to be wide enough so cars can pass? Will you require extra parking? Would you like a circular driveway? A basketball court?

• Will the patio be used for entertaining? Will it be a family or adult area, or both? How much furniture will you use? Should it be accessible from a particular part of the house?

• Do you have existing or future landscaping that needs to be considered?

• Would you like to incorporate special touches, like a retaining wall, a small koi pond, or a stone archway?

If you're working with a full-service landscape professional, and hardscape is part of the landscape design, be certain a hardscape expert will do the installation. A specialist's engineering expertise and product knowledge are vital to the top quality result you want. ■

WHY YOU NEED AN ARBORIST

It's not just your kids, dogs and the neighborhood squirrels trampling through your yard during construction. Excavation equipment, heavy trucks and work crews can spell disaster for your trees. Call an arborist before any equipment is scheduled to arrive and let him develop a plan that will protect the trees, or remove them if necessary.

Landscape
Architects

PETER BOCHENEK AND ASSOCIATES ....**(919) 968-4200**
P.O. Box 16471, Chapel Hill
See Ad on Page: 248, 249
Principal/Owner: Peter Bochenek
Website: www.pbassoc.com e-mail: pb@pbassoc.com
Fax: (919) 968-0360

TG & R LANDSCAPE GROUP ....**(803) 325-1010**
215 S. Hampton Street, Suite 120, Rock Hill
See Ad on Page: 246
Principal/Owner: D. Scott Reister
Website: www.tgrlandscape.com e-mail: tgrlandscape@comporium.net
Fax: (803) 980-8808

WEST FOURTH LANDSCAPE ARCHITECTURE, PA ....**(336) 725-2033**
P.O. Box 20399, Winston-Salem
See Ad on Page: 247
Principal/Owner: Roy H. Pender RLA
Website: e-mail: West Fourth@EarthLink.net
Additional Information: For 22 years, West Fourth has offered personal services
and quality design that our clients demand and deserve.
Fax: (336) 725-5041

ZIMMERMAN/LINDBERG LANDSCAPE ARCHITECTURE ....**(704) 332-9184**
310 East Boulevard, Suite C9, Charlotte
See Ad on Page: 245
Principal/Owner: Brian Zimmerman & Keith Lindberg
e-mail: zimlin@attglobal.net
Fax: (704) 332-8217

Photo by Douglas Palmer

ZIMMERMAN • LINDBERG
landscape architecture
704-332-9184

Assimilating the art of
landscape architecture
and the construction of fine
craftsmen to produce gardens
of serenity and sanctuary.

Landscape
Architecture

•

Landscape
Construction

Rock Hill
803.325.1010

www.tgrlandscape.com

Charlotte
704.525.3300

Peter Bochenek & Associates

Peter Bochenek RLA, ASLA
Landscape Architecture / Project Coordination
Chapel Hill, NC
919.968.4200
www.pbassoc.com

Landscape **Contractors**

A & A PLANTS, NURSERY & LANDSCAPING...................................**(336) 656-7881**
5392 NC 150 East, Brown Summit   Fax: (336) 656-9968
See Ad on Page: 266
<u>Principal/Owner:</u> Rick Apple
<u>Website:</u> www.aaplants.com <u>e-mail:</u> rapple656@aol.com

GARDEN WORLD INC....**(704) 536-2529**
6640 East W.T. Harris Blvd., Suite B , Charlotte
See Ad on Page: 261
<u>Principal/Owner:</u> Richard Allen
<u>Additional Information:</u> Creating elegant landscapes, where attention to detail
makes the difference.

GREENSBORO LANDSCAPE DESIGNERS ....**(336) 275-8006**
PO Box 4951, Greensboro
See Ad on Page: 252

ISLAND DESIGN, LLC....**(704) 455-4833**
PO Box 875, Harrisburg
See Ad on Page: 264
<u>Principal/Owner:</u> Wade Drye

THE MORGAN LANDSCAPE GROUP, INC. ....**(704) 588-2292**
5127 Sandy Porter Rd., Charlotte   Fax: (704) 588-1998
See Ad on Page: 262, 263
<u>Principal/Owner:</u> Mark A. Morgan
<u>Website:</u> www.morganlandscapegroup.com <u>e-mail:</u> morganlandscape@aol.com
<u>Additional Information:</u> 21 Years of experience in the landscape industry.

STONE'S LANDSCAPING ....**(704) 596-4408**
4825 Holly Vista Drive, Charlotte   Fax: (704) 596-4213
See Ad on Page: 251
<u>Principal/Owner:</u> Richard & Charlotte Whetstone

TREELINE LANDSCAPING & NURSERY, INC. ....**(336) 643-4827**
7815 Athens Rd., Stokesdale   Fax: (336) 643-4827
See Ad on Page: 265
<u>Principal/Owner:</u> Mark Lawson
<u>e-mail:</u> treeline@bellsouth.net

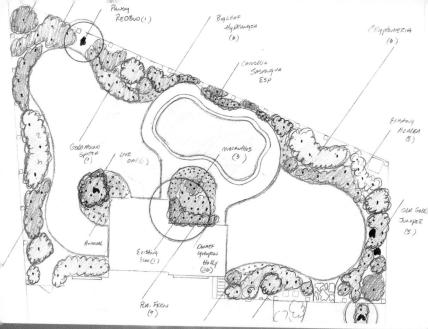

Landscaping Your **Dream** Home

An important part of your dream home will be your outside surroundings, so, of course, you will want a beautiful landscape to complement your home. A great deal of thought will need to go into your landscaping project – this type of project does not solely consist of planting gorgeous flowers or deciding where to place trellises. The following guide will give you an idea of the steps and time that go into landscaping an upscale residential project.

Project
Description

Landscaping an upscale, one-acre property, single family home. This project includes the installation of a swimming pool, masonry walls, fence, lighting, brick paving, a patio, and an assortment of shade trees and plants.

In
Conclusion

The actual completion of a landscaping project varies greatly – a small project could take as little as one week and a large project can take as long as one year. There is no definite timeframe for a project like this. Talk to your landscaper in the initial interviewing and hiring process about timeframes. Ask if you can speak with past clients to find out how long their projects took to complete. This is not a small aspect of the overall completion of your dream home. Therefore, plan on dedicating a significant amount of time to the landscaping of your home. Eventually you will have a finished product that you can be proud of for years to come!

Special thanks to the American Society of Landscape Architects and Van Zelst Inc., Wadsworth, Illinios, for their contribution to this timeline and to Linda Oyama Bryan for her photography.

Distinctive
Landscapes
for
Discriminating
Tastes

704-536-2529
Serving Charlotte
and
Surrounding Areas

GARDEN WORLD LANDSCAPING

The Morgan Landscape Group is an upscale residential landscape firm implementing the best designs in the business . They enjoy a high level of customer responsiveness as the firm takes projects from concept to completion, and into an ongoing landscape management program.

Designs that complement the grounds of Charlotte's most refined homes.

The Morgan
Landscape Group

Creating Outdoor Living Spaces

Specializing In:

- Design Build Landscaping
  Residential
  Commercial
- Irrigation Systems
- Outdoor Lighting
- Hardscapes
  Rock Walls, Pavers,
  Patios & Driveways
- Specimen Nursery Stock

Treeline Landscaping & Nursery, Inc.

7815 Athens Road • Stokesdale, NC 27357

Phone: (336) 643-4827
Email:treeline@bellsouth.net

Realize your Dream Garden

A&A PLANTS

5392 N.C. 150 EAST • BROWN SUMMIT, NC 27214

(336) 656-7881 • Fax (336) 656-9968

www.aaplants.com

Swimming Pools,
Spas & Sport

ESTATE GOLF BY OSBORN ....**(864) 877-2535**
125 Sunbelt Court, Greer   Fax: (864) 877-5859
See Ad on Page: 268
<u>Principal/Owner:</u> James G. Osborn
<u>Website:</u> www.estategolf.com <u>e-mail:</u> estgolf@infi.net
<u>Additional Information:</u> The southeast's oldest premier designer/builder of custom built putting greens with utmost attention to detail in the finest homes.

HEAVENLY BACKYARDS BY SPORT COURT...................................**(704) 821-1890**
13716-D East Independence Blvd., Indian Trail   Fax: (704) 821-1892
See Ad on Page: 269
<u>Principal/Owner:</u> Richard F. Goebel/Mike Linn
<u>Website:</u> www.realpages.com/sites/sportcourt

The Ultimate Putting Green

Bring the pleasure and prestige of an Estate Golf
Putting green to your property:
A surface of unparalleled performance and beauty
that enhances the most elegant landscape.

Toll-free: 888-641-7888 www.estategolf.com

125 Sunbelt Ct.
Greer, SC 29650

SPORT COURT®

Game Courts and Basketball Courts

Home Golf Centers Putting Green

The Ultimate Backyard Sport System
for The Serious Players

Heavenly Backyards
704-821-1890
heavenlysc@earthlink.net

Hardscape, Masonry &
Water Gardens

BELGARD/OLDCASTLE ....**(800) 446-7421**
  PO Box 14489, Greensboro
  See Ad on Page: 234, 272, 273, 280
  <u>Principal/Owner:</u> Billy Patterson
  <u>Website:</u> www.belgardhardscapes.com
Fax: (336) 375-8259

CREATIVE PAVERS, INC. ....**(336) 668-4376**
  3206 Edgefield Dr., Suite #15, Greensboro
  See Ad on Page: 276, 277
  <u>Principal/Owner:</u> Chad Payton
  <u>Website:</u> www.creativepavers.com <u>e-mail:</u> cpavers@bellsouth.net
  <u>Additional Information:</u> Creative Pavers, Inc. has been installing quality outdoor living
  areas, driveways, and segmental retaining walls in North Carolina since 1995.
Fax: (336) 668-4027

EXTERIOR EXPRESSIONS...**(704) 708-5898**
  1508 Industrial Dr, Matthews
  See Ad on Page: 232, 233, 396
Fax: (704) 708-5899

HARD SCAPES..**(704) 759-0320**
  4101 Bon Rea Drive, Charlotte
  See Ad on Page: 271
  <u>Principal/Owner:</u> Adam Simpson
  <u>Website:</u> www.hardscapes.com

MIC & WHICK'S LANDSCAPING, INC. ....**(336) 727-0232**
  200-A Peddycord Park Ct., Kernersville
  See Ad on Page: 274, 275
  <u>Principal/Owner:</u> Alan Whicker and Chris Gibby
  <u>Website:</u> micandwhickslandscaping.com <u>e-mail:</u> micnwhick@yadtel.net
  <u>Additional Information:</u> Specialize in recreating the beauty of nature for our clients.
Fax: (336) 724-5323

are our favorite subjects

Your Custom Landscaping Specialists!

336-727-0232
www.micandwhickslandscaping.com

Mic & Whick's Landscaping Inc.

336•727•0232

Nature at it's Best!

3206 Edgefield Dr. Suite #15
Greensboro, NC 27409
Phone: 336-668-4376
Fax: 336-668-4027
Email:Cpavers@bellsouth.net
www.Creativepavers.com

Decks, Conservatories &
Architectural Elements

ARCHITECTURAL CONCEPT STONE ....**(803) 802-0686**
9072 Northfield Drive, Fort Mill   Fax: (803) 802-1765
See Ad on Page: 279, 394, 395
<u>Principal/Owner:</u> Kevin Sexton
<u>Website:</u> www.arcconceptstone.com
<u>Additional Information:</u> Custom architectural precast featuring decks, copings,
fireplaces, columns, window surrounds, sills, and anything you design.

BELGARD/OLDCASTLE ....**(800) 446-7421**
PO Box 14489, Greensboro   Fax: (336) 375-8259
See Ad on Page: 234, 272, 273, 280
<u>Principal/Owner:</u> Billy Patterson
<u>Website:</u> www.belgardhardscapes.com

ARCHITECTURAL CONCEPT STONE

9072 Northfield Dr. • Fort Mill, NC 29715
803.802.0686 • fax: 803.802.1765

Landscape
Lighting

NIGHTSCAPES LANDSCAPE LIGHTING & DESIGN ....**(704) 875-8785**
114-E Old Statesville Rd., Huntersville   Fax: (704) 875-1785
See Ad on Page: 282, 283
<u>Principal/Owner:</u> Jim Poplin
<u>Website:</u> www.nightscapesdesign.com <u>e-mail:</u> nightscapes1@aol.com
<u>Additional Information:</u> Members of (ALCA) Associated Landscape Contractors
of America. Members of (ASLA) American Society of Landscape Architects.
Members of (NLSLA) North Carolina Society of Landscape Architects.

SHAMROCK LANDSCAPE LIGHTING ....**(336) 784-4436**
4017 Capian Way Court, Winston-Salem
See Ad on Page: 284
<u>Principal/Owner:</u> Joseph A. Donnelly

Superior Style

Beauty

Elegance

WATERGARDENS & FALLS

ARCHITECTURAL DESIGNS

FOUNTAINS

Facinate With Light...

Illuminate By Night

COMMERCIAL & RESIDENTIAL
LANDSCAPING

NIGHTSCAPES
Landscape Lighting & Design

This home done for the firm of Gary Jobe Builder at 2001 Showcase of Homes, Greensboro, NC.

Shamr☘ck
Landscape Lighting

Add Safety, Security & Curb Appeal To Your Property

We Install Floodlights, Garden Lights, Path Lights & Deck Lights
For a FREE Estimate Call Joe Donnelly at 336-785-0388

Location,
Location,
Location!

What better LOCATION for your
advertisement than the
NORTH CAROLINA HOME BOOK!

Just as our readers realize how important
location is when choosing a home, we realize
that it's just as important to you when
allocating your advertising dollars.
That's why we have successfully positioned the
NORTH CAROLINA HOME BOOK to reach
the high-end consumers you want as clients.

**Call 704-549-3687 to find out about our
unique marketing programs and
advertising opportunities.**

Published by
The Ashley Group
8420 University Executive
Suite 810
Charlotte, NC 28262
704.549.3687 fax: 704.549.3695
E-mail: ashleybooksales@cahners.com

Finally...
North Carolina's Own
Home & Design
Sourcebook

The **North Carolina Home Book** is your final destination when searching for home remodeling, building and decorating resources. This comprehensive, hands-on sourcebook to building, remodeling, decorating, furnishing and landscaping a luxury home is required reading for the serious and discriminating homeowner. With more than 500 full-color, beautiful pages, the **North Carolina Home Book** is the most complete and well-organized reference to the home industry. This hardcover volume covers all aspects of the process, includes listings of hundreds of industry professionals, and is accompanied by informative and valuable editorial discussing the most recent trends. Ordering your copy of the **North Carolina Home Book** now can ensure that you have the blueprints to your dream home, in your hand, today.

O R D E R   F O R M

THE NORTH CAROLINA HOME BOOK

☐ YES, please send me _____ copies of the NORTH CAROLINA HOME BOOK at $39.95 per book, plus $3 Shipping & Handling per book.

Total amount enclosed: $_____ Please charge my: ☐ VISA ☐ MasterCard ☐ American Express

Card # _____ Exp. Date _____

Name _____ Phone: ( ) _____

Address _____ E-mail: _____

City _____ State _____ Zip Code _____

Send order to: Attn: Marketing Department—The Ashley Group, 1350 E. Touhy Ave., Suite 1E, Des Plaines, Illinois 60018
Or Call Toll Free: 888-458-1750 Fax: 847-390-2902 E-mail ashleybooksales@cahners.com

All orders must be accompanied by check, money order or credit card # for full amount.

create a showplace expressing your lifestyle

Triangle Design Kitchens partners with the industry's finest artisans and suppliers to offer you one-of-a-kind hand-carvings, exotic veneers, concrete and Pyrolave lava stone countertops, gourmet appliances, unique accessories, and an array of cabinetry from traditional to modern.

Bill Camp, CKD and the design team at Triangle Design Kitchens combine their talents with these partnerships to make your next kitchen a beautiful and functional extension of your image and lifestyle.

Call to make the kitchen you imagine a reality.

Triangle Design Kitchens™

5216 Holly Ridge Drive
Raleigh, North Carolina 27612
phone: 919.787.0256   toll free: 888.251.5182

visit our online showroom at www.TriangleDesignKitchens.com

Form, Function... Fabulous!

Kitchens and baths were once designed for efficiency, with little attention to beauty. Today they are paramount to a home's comfort and style, places to nurture body and spirit.

Without a doubt, today's larger kitchen is the real family room, the heart and soul of the home. Some kitchens serve as the control center in "Smart Houses" wired with the latest technology. With the kitchen as a focal point of the home, good design means the room must be both functional and a pleasure to be in, while reflecting the "feel" of the rest of the home. From the European "unfitted" look to super-high tech, there are styles and finishes to make everyone feel at home in the kitchen.

The bath has evolved into a truly multipurpose "cocooning" area as well. Sufficient room for exercise equipment, spacious master closets, and spa features are all in high demand, resulting in master suites to allow one to escape from the world. The emphasis on quality fixtures and luxury finishes remains, whatever the size of the room.

Photo courtesy of **Dina Lowery's Studio of Design**
Photo by **Pat Shanklin**

FIVE WAYS TO SPOT A TOP QUALITY KITCHEN OR BATH

1. A feeling of timelessness: Sophisticated solutions that blend appropriately with the home's overall architecture and smoothly incorporate new products and ideas.
2. A hierarchy of focal points: Visual elements designed to enhance – not compete with – each other.
3. Superior functionality: Rooms clearly serve the needs they were designed to meet, eliminate traffic problems and work well years after installation.
4. Quality craftsmanship: All elements, from cabinets, counters, and floors, to lighting, windows and furnishings, are built and installed at the highest level of quality.
5. Attention to detail: Thoughtful planning is evident – from the lighting scheme to the practical surfaces to the gorgeous cabinet detailing.

PLANNED TO PERFECTION
THE CUSTOM KITCHEN & BATH

In many ways, the kitchen and bath define how we live and dictate the comfort we enjoy in our everyday lives. Families continue to design their kitchens to be the heart of the home – in every way. It's the central gathering place. It's a work space. It's a command center for whole house electronic control systems. Bathrooms become more luxurious, more multi-functional. Having experienced the pleasures of pampering on vacations, in spas, beauty salons, and health clubs, sophisticated area homeowners are choosing to enjoy a high degree of luxury every day in their own homes.

Homeowners building a new home, or remodeling an existing one, demand flexible and efficient spaces, custom designed to fill their needs. Reaching that goal is more challenging than ever. As new products and technologies race to keep up with the creative design explosion, the need for talented, experienced kitchen and bath designers continues to grow.

The kitchen/bath designer will be a member of your home building team, which also includes the architect, contractor, interior designer and, in new home construction, the landscape architect.

Professional kitchen and bath designers, many of whom are also degreed interior designers, possess the education and experience in space planning particular to kitchens and baths. They can deliver a functional design perfectly suited to your family, while respecting your budget and your wishes. Their understanding of ergonomics, the relationship between people and their working environments, and a familiarity with current products and applications, will be invaluable to you as you plan.

SEARCH OUT AND VALUE
DESIGN EXCELLENCE

Designing a kitchen or bath is an intimate undertaking, filled with many decisions based on personal habits and family lifestyle. Before you select the kitchen/bath professional who will lead you through the project, make a personal commitment to be an involved and interested client. Since the success of these rooms is so important to the daily lives of your family, it's a worthwhile investment of your time and energy.

Choose a designer whose work shows creativity and a good sense of planning. As in any relationship, trust and communication are the foundations for success. Is the designer open to your ideas, and does he or she offer information on how you can achieve your vision? If you can't express your ideas freely, don't enter into a contractual relationship, no matter how much you admire this person's work. If these rooms aren't conceived to fulfill your wishes, your time and resources will be wasted.

What also is true, however, is that professional designers should be given a comfortable degree of latitude to execute your wishes as best as they know how. Accomplished designers earned their reputation by creating beautiful rooms that work, so give their ideas serious consideration for the best overall result.

Many homeowners contact a kitchen or bath designer a year before a project is scheduled to begin. Some come with a full set of complete drawings they simply want to have priced out. Some take full advantage of the designer's expertise and contract for plans drawn from scratch. And some want something in between. Be sure a designer offers the level of services you want – from 'soup to nuts' or strictly countertops and cabinetry.

Designers charge a design fee which often will be used as a deposit if you choose to hire them. If you expect very detailed sets of drawings, including floor plans, elevations, and pages of intricate detail, such as the support systems of kitchen islands, the toe kick and crown molding detail, be specific about your requirements. All contracts should be written, detailed and reviewed by your attorney.

TURNING DREAMS INTO DESIGNS— GET YOUR NOTEBOOK OUT

The first step toward getting your ideas organized is to put them on paper. Jot down notes, tape photos into your Idea Notebook, mark pages of your Home Book. The second step is defining your lifestyle. Pay close attention to how you use the kitchen and bath. For example, if you have a four-burner stove, how often do you cook with all four burners? Do you need a cook surface with more burners, or could you get by with less, freeing up space for a special wok cooking module or more counter space? How often do you use your bathtub? Many upper-end homeowners are forgoing the tub in favor of the multi-head shower surround and using bathtub space for a dressing or exercise area or mini-kitchen. As you evaluate your lifestyle, try to answer questions like these:

THINKING ABOUT KITCHEN DESIGN

• What feeling do you want to create in the kitchen? Traditional feel of hearth and home? The clean, uncluttered lines of contemporary design?

• Is meal preparation the main function of the kitchen? Gourmet cooks and gardeners want a different level of functionality than do homeowners

THE LATEST APPLIANCES

There's a revolution in kitchen appliances, guaranteed to make your life simpler and more enjoyable: High-performance stainless steel cook-top ranges with a commercial level of performance; Cook-tops with interchangeable cooking modules (like woks, griddles); Down draft ventilation on gas cook-tops; Convection ovens with oversize capacity, and electronic touchpad controls; Refrigeration products and systems you can put wherever you could put a cabinet or drawer; Flush-design appliances; Ultra-quiet dish-washers with stainless steel interiors; Refrigerators that accept decorative door panels and handles to match your cabinets; State-of-the-art warming drawers.

293

One Person's Project Estimate:

Ingredients of a New Kitchen

It's fun to imagine, but what might it actually cost to undertake a project described in this chapter? The example below describes a typical project and gives a general estimate of the costs involved.

PROJECT DESCRIPTION

Designing and installing a high-end, kitchen, 16' x 33' sq. ft.

Consultation: retainer, applied towards cabinet purchase $2,500

Cabinetry $44,000

> Kitchen, Island, Pantry, Desk
> 36"- 42" high wall cabinets to ceiling
> Maple w/med. stain, modified Shaker styling, custom solid wood construction
> Cabinet Accessories
>
> To allow for an ergonomic, efficient use of space, roll-out shelves, an appliance garage, a lazy susan, a trash pull-out, cutlery dividers, tray dividers, a tip-out at sink and cabinet hardware were incorporated.

Glass $3,500

> Stained glass doors, glass shelves

Countertop $12,000

> Granite, 1" thick, large beveled edge

Backsplash $2,500

> Tumbled marble with accent mosaic

Appliance Package, all stainless steel $20,000

> 36" gas cooktop with hood
> Two electric ovens, 48" built-in refrigerator,
> Two dishwashers, under counter refrigerator,
> Warming drawer, microwave, disposal, hot water dispenser

Plumbing Fixtures $2,900

> Undermount double bowl main sink, prep sink,
> pull-out faucets, soap dispensers, water filter system

Flooring $4,000

> Stone-look porcelain tile

Lighting $2,500

> General, task, accent, combination of low voltage, halogen and xenon

Labor $7,000

> Installation of cabinets, appliances, counters,
> and backsplash. Room preparation, floor installation,
> electric and plumbing hook-ups, by general contractor.

TOTAL...$98,400

294

Note: A very similar look can be had at several price points. For a less expensive installation, custom cabinets can be replaced with stock or semi-custom. The granite tops could be made of butcher block or laminate. Clear or frosted glass can be substituted for custom glass. Depending on the choice of materials, prices could be cut back by half the quoted cost.

Maple kitchen cabinets- modified shaker style

Under-mounted sink

Granite countertop - beveled edge

WHAT DESIGNERS OFFER YOU

1. Access to the newest products: With their considerable knowledge of products and solutions, your remodeling or budget limitations can be more easily addressed.

2. Ergonomic design for a custom fit: Designers consider all the measurements – not just floor plan space – but also how counter and cabinet height and depth measure up to the needs of the individual family members.

3. A safe environment: Safety is the highest priority. As kitchens and baths serve more functions, managing traffic for safety's sake becomes more crucial.

4. Orderly floor plans: When an open refrigerator door blocks the path from the kitchen to the breakfast room, or you're bumping elbows in the bathroom, poor space planning is the culprit.

5. Smart storage: Ample storage in close proximity to appropriate spaces is essential.

who eat out often or want to be in and out of the kitchen quickly.

• How does the family use the kitchen? How will their needs change your requirements over the next ten years? (If you can't imagine the answer to this question, ask friends who are a few years ahead of you in terms of family life.)

• Do you want easy access to the backyard, dining room, garage?

• Is there a special view you want preserved or established?

• Do you want family and friends to be involved and close to the action in the kitchen?

• What appliances and amenities must be included? Do some research on this question. Warming drawers, refrigeration zones, wine coolers, ultra-quiet dishwashers that sense how dirty the dishes are, cooktops with interchangeable cooking modules, convection ovens with electronic touchpad controls, are all available.

• What are your storage needs? If you own a lot of kitchen items, have a relatively small kitchen, or want personally tailored storage space, ask your kitchen designer to take a detailed inventory of your possessions. Top quality cabinets can be customized to fit your needs. Kitchen designers, custom cabinet makers, or space organization experts can guide you. Consider custom options such as:

- Slotted storage for serving trays
- Pull-out recycling bins
- Plate racks and wine racks
- Cutlery dividers
- Angled storage drawer for spices
- Pivoting shelving systems
- Pull-out or elevator shelves for food processors, mixers, televisions or computers

• Is the kitchen also a work area or home office? Do you need a location for a computerized home management or intercom system?

THINKING ABOUT BATH DESIGN

• What look are you trying to create? Victorian, Colonial, contemporary, whimsical?

• What functions must it fill? Exercise area, sitting room, dressing or make-up area?

• Who will use the bath? Children, teens, guests, (and how many)?

- What is the traffic pattern? How do people move in and around a bathroom? (Set up your video camera in the corner one morning to get a realistic view.)

- What amenities are desired? Luxury shower systems, whirlpool tub, ceiling heat lamps, heated towel bars, spa, heated tile floors, audio and telephone systems

- What are your storage needs? Linen or clothes closets? Stereo and CD storage? Professionals will customize spaces for your needs.

- Do you want hooks for towels or bathrobes? Heated towel bars or rings?

THE SKY'S THE LIMIT

New high-end kitchen budgets can easily reach the $100,000 range, so it's important to identify your specific needs and wishes. The sky's the limit when designing and installing a luxury kitchen or bath in the 2000s, so don't get caught by surprise by the cost of high quality cabinetry, appliances and fixtures. Know what you're willing to spend and make sure your designer is aware of your budget. Projects have a way of growing along the way. If you've established a realistic budget, you have a solid way to keep the project moving forward and prioritizing your wishes. As you establish your budget, think in terms of this general breakdown of expenses:

Cabinets	40%
Appliances	15%
Faucets and Fixtures	8%
Flooring	7%
Windows	7%
Countertops	8%
Labor	15%

THE NEW KITCHEN – THE FLAVOR OF THE PAST – A TASTE OF THE FUTURE

Many of the fabulous new kitchens being built now don't look "new." The desire for an inviting, lived-in look that encourages friends and family to linger over coffee and conversation is leading homeowners to embrace European design ideas of furniture-quality cabinetry and dedicated work zones. Consumers are investing in restaurant-quality appliances, gorgeous imported natural stone countertops and floors, and luxury options like dedicated wine coolers, stem glass holders, and plate racks. Tastes are turning to more classical, traditional detailing in cabinetry, with Georgian, Greek and Roman influence in its architecture.

"WHAT ABOUT RESALE?"

This is a question designers hear when homeowners individualize their kitchens and baths. It's only prudent to consider the practical ramifications of any significant investment, including investing in a new custom kitchen and bath. Beautiful upscale kitchens and baths will only enhance the value of your home. Indeed, these two rooms are consistently credited with recouping much of their original cost. Research by professional builders' organizations and real estate companies bears this out year after year. The greatest return, however, is in the present, in the enjoyment of the space.

YOUR KITCHEN.COM

Technology has arrived in the kitchen. On-line grocery shopping, computers, multiple phone lines, intercom, security system and "smart house" controls. Right by the breakfast table.

This is not to say that homeowners no longer demand state-of-the-art features; quite the contrary. New, smart ideas play an ever more important role in a kitchen's daily life. Kitchens are often equipped as a central hub in a computer automated home, with everything from ovens and entertainment systems accessible by remote control. Home office or homework areas equipped with telephones, computers, printers, and fax machines are included in most every new project. With advances in refrigeration technology, homeowners now have separate integrated refrigerators and freezer drawers installed near the appropriate work zone – a refrigerated vegetable drawer near the sink, a freezer drawer by the microwave, dedicated refrigerators to keep grains or cooking oils at their perfect temperatures. Ultra-quiet dishwashers, instant hot water dispensers, roll-out warming drawers and versatile cooktops are just some of the products that meet the demands of today's luxury lifestyle.

THE NEW BATH – PRACTICALITY DRENCHED WITH PANACHE AND POLISH

Imagine it's a Thursday night at the end of a very busy week. You come home, have a great work out while listening to your favorite CDs over the loudspeakers in your private exercise room, then jump into an invigorating shower where multiple shower heads rejuvenate your tired muscles, and a steaming, cascading waterfall pulls all the stress from your body. You wrap yourself in a big fluffy bath sheet, toasty from the brass towel warmer, as you step onto the ceramic tile floor that's been warmed by an underfloor radiant heating unit. You grab something comfortable from your lighted, walk-in closet, and then head out of your luxurious bathroom to the kitchen to help with dinner.

A master bath such as this, built in custom luxury homes, fills a growing demand for private retreats replete with nurturing indulgences.

Master bathrooms are being rethought, with the emphasis shifting from form to function. These baths are still large, up to 400 square feet, but the space is organized differently. The newly defined master bath is actually an extension of the master suite, often including his and her walk-in closets, mirrored exercise space, (in remodeling projects, carved out of a spare bedroom) and separate areas for dressing, applying make-up, listening to music or making coffee.

Large whirlpool tubs are often replaced with custom shower systems with built-in seats and steam capabilities. Other stylish alternatives are Victorian style claw-foot tubs, or smaller whirlpool tubs.

A STEP UP

Custom counter height is an idea whose time has arrived in new and remodeled homes in North Carolina. Multiple heights, appropriate to the task or the people using the particular area, are common. When one permanent height doesn't work as a solution to a problem, consider asking for a step to be built into the toe kick panel of the cabinetry.

GET TWO DISHWASHERS

Homeowners today are installing extra dishwashers:
1. To make clean up after a party a one-night affair.
2. To serve as a storage cabinet for that extra set of dishes. They're also installing dishwashers at a more friendly height to eliminate unnecessary bending.

THE REALITY OF REMODELING

Dollar-smart homeowners know that in cost versus value surveys, kitchen renovations and bath additions or renovations yield a very high return on the original investment. These homeowners rarely embark on such remodeling projects with resale in mind. However, knowing their investment is a wise one gives them the freedom to fully realize their dreams of the ultimate sybaritic bath or the friendliest family kitchen that accommodates them now and well into the future.

For more information on remodeling, see "The Second Time's The Charm" in the Custom Home Builders and Remodelers section.

CONTEXTUALISM IN THE KITCHEN AND BATH

Like any other rooms in the home, continuity and contextualism in the kitchen and bath are important to the overall appearance of the home. This is an important point to consider in a remodeling project, especially in an historic home. There often are restrictions on the materials and structural changes that may be made in historic buildings. Your kitchen or bath designer should be aware of these kinds of restrictions.

A REMODELING CONTINGENCY FUND

Kitchen and bath remodeling projects are well known for unexpected, unforeseen expenses, so put a contingency fund in your budget from the beginning. This fund can cover anything from structural changes to your sudden desire to install skylights in the kitchen.

THE BEAUTY OF TOP QUALITY SURFACES

Luxury surfaces continue to add astonishing beauty to kitchens and baths in new and remodeled homes throughout the area. Solid surfaces now are available in an ever-widening range of colors, including a granite look, with high degrees of translucence and depth. Granite and stone add a beautiful, natural look, with an abundance of choices and finishes. Tile, stainless steel, laminates, and wood – even concrete – are other possibilities. Each surface has its benefits, beyond the inherent beauty it can add to your design.

Your kitchen designer will advise you on the best choices for your project, based on overall design and budget. Use the professionals showcased in these pages to find the best quality materials and craftsmanship. ■

TAKING A TEST DRIVE

You wouldn't invest in a new car without taking it out for a test drive, so take the opportunity up front to test the individual fixtures and elements of a new kitchen or bath. Don't be hesitant to grab a magazine and climb into a bathtub, or to test sit a number of possible toilet choices or shower seats. Take your family to a showroom to evaluate counter heights and faucets. The more involved you can be in the planning, the more fun you'll have, and the better the end result will be.

299

Kitchen & Bath
Designers

AMERICAN KITCHENS, INC. ....**(704) 364-1448**
1112 McAlway Rd., Charlotte
See Ad on Page: 318, 319

CAROLINA KITCHEN STUDIOS..**(919) 870-9202**
6616-201 Six Forks Road, Raleigh
See Ad on Page: 306
Fax: (919) 870-7646
Principal/Owner: Lynn Thomas
Website: www.carolinakitchenstudios.com e-mail: CarolinaKitchens@aol.com

CHARLOTTE CABINETS INC....**(704) 331-9690**
1920 Cleveland Ave., Charlotte
See Ad on Page: 304, 305
Fax: (704) 331-9691
Principal/Owner: Scott Knowles
Website: www.charlottecabinets.com e-mail: charcabs@bellsouth.net
Additional Information: Exclusive dealer of Poggenpohl, Heritage Custom Cabinetry, and Elmwood Kitchens.

COLLINS & COMPANY ....**(240) 747-1600**
10539 Metropolitan Ave, Kensington
See Ad on Page: 318, 319
Fax: (301) 946-7869
Principal/Owner: Scott Collins

CUSTOM CABINETRY ....**(336) 767-8156**
668 Old Hollow Road, Winston-Salem
See Ad on Page: 320, 321
Fax: (336) 767-9028
Principal/Owner: Paul Jurgens
e-mail: pwjurgens@aol.com

DCI KITCHEN AND BATH ....**(704) 926-6000**
1300 South Boulevard Suite C, Charlotte
See Ad on Page: 302, 303
Fax: (704) 926-6001
Principal/Owner: Carol Lindell
Website: www.cabinetsbyDCI.com e-mail: caroll@cabinetsbyDCI.com
Additional Information: Providing the highest quality in cabinetry, design services, installation, and customer attention. Ensuring each client enjoys an exceptional home.

HAILEY COMPANY LLC...**(828) 459-7307**
5024 Bolick Road, Claremont
See Ad on Page: 301
Fax: (828) 459-1144
Principal/Owner: Cecil Hollifield
Website: www.haileycompany.com e-mail: TheHaileyCompany@aol.com

HAMPTON KITCHENS OF RALEIGH, INC. ....**(919) 850-0366**
5024 Old Wake Forest Rd., Raleigh
See Ad on Page: 318, 319

J & J CUSTOM KITCHENS & BATHS, INC. ....**(336) 272-6255**
523 N. Cedar St, Greensboro
See Ad on Page: 318, 319

KITCHEN & BATH DESIGN CENTER ....**(803) 329-2969**
2424 India Hook Rd., Suite 160, Rock Hill
See Ad on Page: 318, 319

KITCHEN & BATH GALLERIES..**(919) 783-7100**
8411 Glenwood Ave, Raleigh
See Ad on Page: 318, 319

KITCHEN & BATH GALLERIES..**(919) 806-1544**
105 West NC 54, Suite 275, Durham
See Ad on Page: 318, 319

300

continued on page 315

HAILEY COMPANY LLC

5024 BOLICK ROAD CLAREMONT NC 28610
PHONE 828-459-7307 FAX 459-1144

VAN - 01- 00

VAN - 20-30

VAN - 10-34

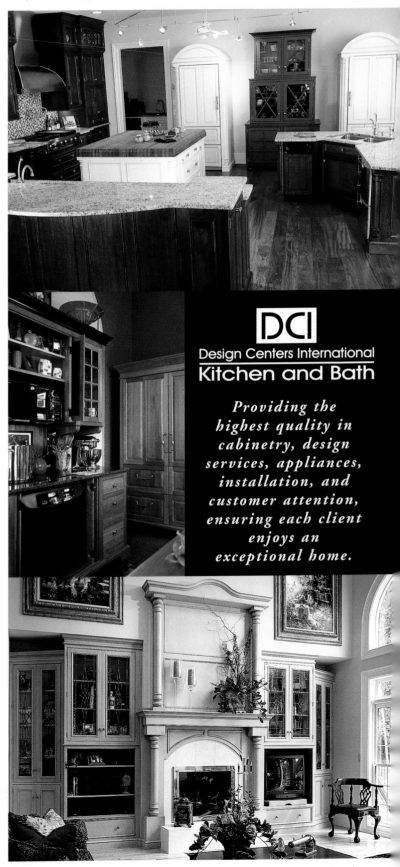

Charlotte Cabinets
Fine Custom Cabinetry

Michael LoBiondo Photographic 2001

When you can have it *exactly* the way you want it

anything less won't do.

PLATO

Building Your **Dream** Kitchen and Bath

Y ou may live in a house you love, in a neighborhood that suits you perfectly. However, your home may not fit your changing lifestyle or desires. The following timeline shows the steps involved in planning, executing, and finishing the major remodeling of a kitchen and full bath. It will help you to see the major tasks involved, and give you helpful information to make this process go more smoothly.

Project
Description

The remodeling of a kitchen and full bath. For the kitchen, the cabinets will be replaced, an island added, new flooring installed, and a breakfast nook with a bay window constructed. For the bath, a whirlpool will be installed, new flooring and new countertops will replace the old, and a closet will be carved out of the existing space.

In
Conclusion

The process of remodeling a kitchen and bath can be somewhat mysterious, sometimes perplexing, and often frustrating. At the end of the process, however, will be two of the most beautiful, comfortable, and enjoyable rooms of your home well into the future!

Special thanks to Neff Kitchens (Toronto, Ontario, Canada), the National Association of the Remodeling Industry, Inc. and the Design Guild of Chicago, Illinois for their contributions to this article.

continued from page **300**

KITCHEN & BATH GALLERIES...**(919) 467-6341**
108 East Chatham St., Cary
See Ad on Page: 318, 319

THE KITCHEN CENTER OF CHARLOTTE ....**(704) 372-1209**
1530 East Boulevard, Charlotte
See Ad on Page: 318, 319

KITCHEN CENTER OF WINSTON-SALEM ....**(336) 725-2343**
1105 Burke St, Winston-Salem
See Ad on Page: 318, 319

KITCHEN KREATIONS, INC. ....**(828) 267-0768**
101 Government Ave., SW, Suite , Hickory
See Ad on Page: 318, 319

THE KITCHEN SPECIALIST, INC...**(919) 490-4922**
3407 University Drive, Durham   Fax: (919) 286-4922
See Ad on Page: 316, 318, 319
Principal/Owner: Mary T. Liebhold
e-mail: design@thekitchenspecialist.com

KOEHLER KITCHEN & BATH ....**(336) 275-8402**
1220-A Battleground Ave, Greensboro
See Ad on Page: 318, 319

SANDAVIS CUSTOM KITCHENS ....**(910) 692-7000**
160-E Pinehurst Ave., Southern Pines
See Ad on Page: 318, 319

TRIANGLE DESIGN KITCHENS, INC. ....**(888) 251-5182**
5216 Holly Ridge Drive, Raleigh   Fax: (919) 787-0274
See Ad on Page: 290, 317
Principal/Owner: Bill Camp
Website: www.triangledesignkitchens.com e-mail: info@triangledesignkitchens.com

Fine Design & Cabinetry

The Kitchen Specialist, Inc.
3407 University Dr.• Durham, NC 27707 • 919.490.4922
www.thekitchenspecialist.com

What inspires you?

Perhaps it's a walk in an English garden. Whatever your inspiration, as Wood-Mode design professionals we understand how important the feeling of your new kitchen is to you. Which is why we'll do everything possible to help you achieve the look you want.

RALEIGH, DURHAM, CARY, CHAPEL HILL

KITCHEN & BATH GALLERIES
108 East Chatham Street
Cary, NC 27511
Phone: 919-467-6341

KITCHEN & BATH GALLERIES
105 West NC 54, Suite 275
Durham, NC 27713
Phone: 919-806-1544

THE KITCHEN & SPECIALIST
3407 University Drive
Durham, NC 27707
Phone: 919-490-4922

HAMPTON KITCHENS OF RALEIGH, INC.
5024 Old Wake Forest Road
Raleigh,NC 27609
Phone: 919-850-0366

KITCHEN & BATH GALLERIES
8411 Glenwood Avenue
Raleigh,NC 27612
Phone: 919-783-7100

SOUTHERN PINES

SANDAVIS CUSTOM KITCHENS
160-E Pinehurst Avenue
Southern Pines, NC 28387
Phone: 910-692-7000

WINSTON-SALEM

KITCHEN CENTER OF WINSTON-SALEM
1105 Burke Street
Winston-Salem, NC 27101
Phone: 336-725-2343

Custom Cabinetry

Custom Cabinetry, Inc
668 Old Hollow Road
Winston-Salem, NC
336.767.8156

Kitchen & Bath Design and Consulting
Custom Cabinets and Custom Finishes
Natural Countertops
Custom Entertainment Centers
Home Theater Cabinetry
Personal Studies & Libraries
Custom Mantels
Master Craftsmanship

Kitchen & Bath
Surfaces

MARBLE & GRANITECH, INC. ....**(704) 525-2345**
414 Foster Avenue, Charlotte   Fax: (704) 525-2395
See Ad on Page: 288, 289, 389
Principal/Owner: Jeff Heldreth
Website: www.mgimarblegranite.com

Appliances

BONNIE FLEMING LLC ....**(704) 333-9234**
651 Museum Drive, Charlotte   Fax: (704) 338-9245
See Ad on Page: 325
<u>Principal/Owner:</u> Bonnie Fleming
<u>Website:</u> www.agasales.com <u>e-mail:</u> agasalespr@aol.com

MIELE, INC....**(800) 421-4685**
6741 Bulkley Road, Lorton   Fax: (703) 339-5563
See Ad on Page: 324

Technologically superior function in sleek European form. The real genius of Miele is in the details.

The details provide the ultimate in performance and beauty. Fully integrated dishwashers that disappear in a whisper, laundry systems that provide true fabric care, the revolutionary convection steam oven, and the world's first built-in coffee system are just some of the Miele appliances that have been setting the standards of excellence for over 101 years.

For the dealer nearest you, or for more information, call 1-800-463-0260 or visit miele.com.

Experience the full Miele Collection at one of our showrooms:
Princeton • Beverly Hills • Boca Raton • Wellesley
Northbrook • Dallas • San francisco • Portland

Miele

anything else is a compromise

Looking for the ovens, cooktops, microwave, hood fans, warming drawers, toasters, coffee pots, crock pots, grills, griddles...?

Consider an AGA. From Martha Stewart to Mel Gibson and Paul McCartney, thousands of homeowners worldwide treasure the simplicity and elegance of the legendary AGA cooker.

Why an AGA cooker? Quite simply, it is the world's finest and most complete cooker, taking the place of every cooking appliance in the kitchen.

Outcook, Outlook, Outlive the others.
Experience the AGA, the world's most perfect cooker.

New in the

Photo by **Van Miller**

DCI KITCHEN & BATH

The Luxurious Master Bath:
Revitalize your mind and spirit in your own private hideaway furnished with quality custom cabinetry. Designed and engineered to reflect your special style, this beautiful cabinetry features furniture-inspired details like dove-tailed drawers, dental crown molding and convex reeded columns. Custom designs let you create a boudoir, bath and dressing room as unique as you are.

BONNIE FLEMING, LLC

AGA Companion Stove:
Modeled after the legendary AGA Cooker, the new AGA Companion has the same cast-iron look and AGA quality without size concerns. Measuring only 24 in. wide, it is perfect for small galley kitchens or apartments. The AGA Companion gives homeowners the convenience of electric double ovens, coupled with the speed of four gas burners. An AGA Companion can even be added to large kitchens already outfitted with the AGA Cooker, for even more versatility.

Showroom

Photo by **Jim Green**

THE KITCHEN SPECIALIST, INC.
Integrated Stainless Sinks:
Today's improved finishing techniques make stainless steel counter-tops with custom-designed integrated sinks accessible to the home chef. This sleek, unified design combines the function of a commercial sink with the finish desired in high-end residential applications.

CHARLOTTE CABINETS, INC.
Poggenpohl Aluminum Kitchen:
To Poggenpohl, sense and sensuality are a single unit. They are two inseparable concepts that complement each other beautifully. Together they can provide a kitchen that meets the highest requirements with regard to function, design, material and manufacture. Poggenpohl proves that there is no reason why food preparation should not be as pleasant as eating.

The Ashley Group Luxury Home Resource Collection

The **Ashley Group (www.theashleygroup.com)** is pleased to offer as your final destination when searching for home improvement and luxury resources the following **Home Books** in your local market. Available Now: *Chicago, Washington D.C., South Florida, Los Angeles, Dallas/Fort Worth, Detroit, Colorado, New York, Atlanta, Arizona, Philadelphia, San Diego, North Carolina,* and *Las Vegas*. These comprehensive, hands-on guides to building, remodeling, decorating, furnishing, and landscaping a luxury home, are required reading for the serious and selective homeowner. With over 700 full-color, beautiful pages, the **Home Book** series in each market covers all aspects of the building and remodeling process, including listings of hundreds of local industry professionals, accompanied by informative and valuable editorial discussing the most recent trends.

Order your copies today and make your dream come true!

333

Elegant Touches

Fine, handcrafted interior architectural elements are the details that distinguish the highest quality custom-designed homes. They lend richness and elegance, infusing a home with character and originality. Even an empty room can speak volumes about the personal taste and style of its owners with cabinetry, moldings, ceiling medallions, chair rails, staircases, mirrors and mantels. Windows, doors, and hardware must endure the rigors of regular use, synthesizing beauty and function into high quality design statements made to stand the test of time. Bring your eye for detail as you explore the finest in architectural elements on the following pages.

Photo courtesy of **Interior Trim Creations**

WALL TO WALL ELEGANCE

Nowhere is the commitment to elegant living through quality materials more apparent than in the selection of cabinets and millwork. Representing a significant percentage of the overall cost of a new or renovated home, sophisticated homeowners use this opportunity to declare their dedication to top quality.

Architectural millwork, made to order according to a set of architectural drawings, is becoming an increasingly popular luxury upgrade. Such detailing creates a richly nostalgic atmosphere that reminds homeowners of the comfort and security of a grandparents' home or the elegance of a club they've been in.

Elegant libraries, dens or sitting rooms dressed with fashionable raised panel cabinetry and special moldings are often included in the plans for new homes and remodeling projects. As a homeowner considering how and where to install millwork, ask yourself questions like these:

• How is the room used? Will a study be used for work or for solitude? Entertaining or a second office? Will it have to function as both a working office and an elegant room?

• How are the cabinets and shelves used? Books, collectibles, audio-video equipment, computer, fax or copy machines?

• What look do you want? You may want to consider "dressing" your rooms in different woods. You may like the rich look and feel of cherry paneling in your library, mahogany in the foyer, oak in a guest room and plaster in a dining room.

• Will the interior millwork choices work with the exterior architecture? A colonial home reminiscent of Mount Vernon should be filled with authentic details, like "dog-ear" corners, that create classic luxury. Using millwork inside a modern home can add interest and warmth to one or many rooms.

TIME IS OF THE ESSENCE

Hand-crafted high quality woodwork cannot be rushed. Millwork specialists encourage clients to contact them as early as possible with a clear idea of what kind of architectural statement they wish to make. The earlier you plan these details, the more options you'll have. Wainscoting with raised panels has to be coordinated with electrical outlets, window and door openings; beamed ceilings with light fixtures, and crown moldings with heating vents.

Hold a preliminary meeting before construction begins while it's early enough to incorporate innovative or special requirements into your plans. The more time you can devote to design (two to

PRICING A POWER LIBRARY

• A 15- by 16-foot library, fully paneled in cherry, mahogany or oak, some cabinets, with moldings, desk with hidden computer, coffered ceilings: $20,000 to $30,000.

• In a 16- by 24-foot two-story study, less paneling and more cabinetry of cherry, mahogany or oak, heavy with moldings, and radius work, desk with more pull out and hidden compartments for fax machine, small copier, bar with leaded glass cabinet fronts and a marble top, built-in humidor, and heavily coffered ceilings with multiple steps: $40,000.

three weeks is recommended), the better your result will be. You're creating a custom millwork package that's never been designed for anyone before. Investments made on the front end are the most valuable. Ask about design fees, timelines and costs per revision. Keep your builder up to date on all of your millwork plans.

Drawings can be as detailed as you require. If you want to see the intricacies of a radius molding before you contract for it, let the millwork specialist know your requirements. Ask to see wood samples, with and without stain or paint.

Try to visit installed projects to get a firsthand feel for the quality of a specialist's work and to develop clearer ideas for your own home.

Changes made after an order is placed are costly. Therefore, if you're unsure, don't make a commitment. Add accessory moldings and other details as you see the project taking shape.

Expect a heavily laden room to take at least five to eight weeks to be delivered, about the time from the hanging of drywall to the installation of flooring. Installation takes one to three weeks, depending on the size and scope of the project.

THE ELEGANT REFINEMENT OF CUSTOM CABINETRY

Handcrafted custom cabinets are a recognizable standard of excellence which lend refinement and beauty to a home. Built in a kitchen, library, bathroom, or closet, or as a free-standing entertainment system or armoire, custom cabinets are a sophisticated signature statement.

There are no limits to the possibilities of custom cabinets. The requirements of any space, no matter how unusual, can be creatively met. The endless combinations of style and detail promise unique cabinetry to homeowners who are searching for an individual look, while the first class craftsmanship of experienced, dedicated woodworkers promises unparalleled quality.

DESIGNING HANDSOME CABINETRY

Cabinetry is a major element in your dream home, so let your imagination soar. Collect pictures of cabinets, noting the particular features you like. Cabinet makers appreciate visual examples because it's easier to interpret your desires from pictures than from words. Pictures crystallize your desires.

HOW TO RECOGNIZE CUSTOM CABINET QUALITY

1. **Proper sanding which results in a smooth, beautiful finish.**
2. **Superior detail work, adding unexpected elegance.**
3. **Classic application of design features and architectural details.**
4. **Beautiful, functional hardware selections.**
5. **High-quality hinges and drawer glides.**
6. **Superior overall functionality.**

WHY YOU WANT A PROFESSIONAL DESIGNER

- They rely on experience to deliver you a custom product. Computer tools are great, but nothing replaces the experienced eye.
- They have established relationships with other trades, and can get top-quality glass fronts for your cabinets, or granite for a bar top.
- Their design ability can save you significant dollars in installation.
- They know how

One Person's Project Estimate:

Adding a Winding Elegance

It's fun to imagine, but what might it actually cost to undertake a project described in this chapter? The example below describes a typical project and gives a general estimate of the costs involved.

Project Description

Construction of a high-end, cherry wood circular staircase, 16-rise (stairs)

Scenario I
Staircase is constructed as part of a new home construction, based on previous blueprint renderings.

Raw Materials (lumber)..$ 9,630

Labor (Shop time)..$34,295

Labor (Installation)..$ 4,680

Total:...$48,605

Scenario II
Staircase is constructed as an addition to an existing home.
In addition to the above prices, the following quotes would be added.

Consultation (Quote)..$265

Field measurement..$210
    Job site measurements are taken

Preliminary drawings.. $0

Estimating $360
    Processing the information from a blueprint and
    determining the cost of the raw materials, labor and any
    other type of subtiers (paint, special material).

Proposal $100

Engineering...$360

$50,030

Cherry wood
circular
staircase

Optional
baluster
detail

• What is the exterior style of your home and do you want to continue that style inside?

• How will you the use the cabinets? Cutlery trays, pull-out bins? Shelves for books, CDs, computer software, collections?

• What styles and embellishments do you like? Shaker, Prairie, Country English, Contemporary? Fancy moldings, wainscoting, inlaid banding? Use your Idea Notebook to communicate your preferences.

• Do you prefer particular woods? Cherry, oak, sycamore, or the more exotic ebony, Bubinga or Swiss pearwood? (Species must be selected on the basis of the finish you want.)

• Will cabinetry be visible from other rooms in the house? Must it match previously installed or selected flooring or countertops? (Take samples.)

PRICING OF CUSTOM KITCHEN CABINETS

• Deluxe Kitchen - Face frame-style cabinets of oak, maple or pine, with raised panel doors; crown molding on upper cabinetry, decorative hardware, wood nosing (cap) around counter tops: $10,000 - $20,000
• Upgrade to Shaker inset-style cabinets in cherrywood, painted finish: $20,000 additional.

MANAGING THE LENGTHY PROCESS OF A CUSTOM CABINET PROJECT

With plenty of unhurried time, you can be more creative, while allowing the woodworkers the time they need to deliver a top quality product. Take your blueprints to a cabinet maker early. Although installation occurs in the latter part of the construction, measuring usually takes place very early on.

If your project is carefully thought out, you won't be as likely to change your mind, but a contingency budget of 10 to 15 percent for changes (like adding radiuses or a lacquered finish) is recommended.

Custom cabinets for a whole house, (kitchen, butler's pantry, library, master bath, and three to four additional baths) may take 10 to 15 weeks, depending on the details involved (heavy carving adds significant time). Cabinets for a kitchen remodeling may take two months.

THE DRAMATIC EFFECT OF EXCEPTIONAL STAIRCASES

Take full advantage of the opportunity to upgrade your new or remodeled home with a spectacular staircase by contacting the stairmakers early in the design phase. Their familiarity with products, standards and building codes will be invaluable to you and your architect, contractor or interior designer.

Visit a stair showroom or workroom on your own or with your architect, interior designer or builder during the architectural drawing phase of your project. Discuss how you can achieve what you want at a cost-conscious price. Choosing a standard size radius of 24 inches, in place of a custom 25 1/2 inch radius, for example, will help control costs.

Although your imagination may know no bounds in designing a staircase, hard and fast local building codes may keep your feet on the ground. Codes are not static, and stairmakers constantly update their files on local restrictions regarding details like the rise and run of a stair, and the size and height of rails.

THE STAIR-BUILDING PROCESS

The design of your stairs should be settled in the rough framing phase of the overall building project. If you work within this time frame, the stairs will be ready for installation after the drywall is hung and primer has been applied to the walls in the stair area.

Stairs can be built out of many woods. The most popular choice is red oak, but cherry, maple, walnut and mahogany are also used. If metal railings are preferred, you'll need to contact a specialist.

A top quality stair builder will design your stairs to your specifications. Consider the views you want of the house while on the stairs, and what kind of front entrance presentation you prefer. You may want to see the stairs from a particular room. An expert also can make suggestions regarding comfort and safety, and what styles will enhance the overall architecture.

Plans which are drawn on a computer can be changed with relative ease and can be printed at full size. This is very helpful to homeowners who want to see exactly what the stairs will look like in their home. The full-size plans can be taken to the job site and tacked to the floor to be experienced firsthand.

THE POLISHED ARTISTRY OF CUSTOM GLASS AND MIRROR

A room can be transformed through the use of custom decorative glass and mirrors. Artists design intricately patterned, delicately painted glass to add light and architectural interest in all kinds of room dividers and partitions. Glass artistry can be based on any design, playing on the texture of carpet, the pattern of the brick, or repeating a fabric design. A glass block wall or floor panel can add the touch of distinction that sets a home above the others. Stained glass, usually associated with beautiful classic styling, can be designed in any style – from contemporary to art deco to traditional.

Top specialists, like those presented in the following pages, take great care in designing and delivering unique, top quality products. They work with top quality fabricated products, with the highest quality of beveling and edge work.

USING PLASTER DETAILING

Plaster architectural detailing and trim add a distinctive look to any home. Most often used in out of the way places, like in ceiling medallions or crown moldings, the high relief detailing is especially impressive.

PRICES OF CUSTOM STAIRS

Stairs can cost anywhere from $200 to $95,000, depending on size, materials and the complexity of design:
• Red Oak spiral staircase, upgraded railing: $10,000
• Red Oak circle stairs, standard railings on both sides and around upstairs landing: $13,000
• Six flights of Red Oak circle stairs stacked one atop the next, with landings at the top of each stair: $95,000
• Walnut or mahogany adds 50 percent to the overall cost.

DOOR #1, #2, OR #3?

• **Door #1 - Six panel oak door with sidelights of leaded glass: $1,700 - $2,000**

• **Door #2 - Six panel oak door with lead and beveled glass: $3,000**

• **Door #3 - Oversized, all matched oak, with custom designed leaded glass and brass, sidelights, elliptical top over door: $15,000**

• **Allow $500 to $1,500 for doorknobs, hinges and other hardware.**

THREE TIPS FOR DOOR HARDWARE

**1. Use three hinges to a door - it keeps the door straight.
2. Match all hardware - hinges, knobs, handles, all in the same finish. Use levers or knobs - don't mix.
3. Use a finish that will last.**

THE ARTISTIC PROCESS

Glass specialists will visit your home or building site to make recommendations and estimate costs and delivery time. Study their samples and if they have a showroom, go take a look. Perhaps you could visit an installed project. Seeing the possibilities can stimulate your imagination and open your eyes to new ideas in ways pictures simply cannot.

Allow a month to make a decision and four weeks for custom mirror work delivery, and ten to 14 weeks for decorated glass.

In order to have the glass or mirror ready for installation before the carpet is laid, decisions must be made during the framing or rough construction phase in a new home or remodeling job. Mirrored walls are installed as painting is being completed, so touch-ups can be done while painters are still on site.

Expect to pay a 50 percent deposit on any order after seeing a series of renderings and approving a final choice. Delivery generally is included in the price.

THE DRAMATIC EFFECT OF CUSTOM WINDOWS AND DOORS

Just as we're naturally drawn to establish eye contact with each other, our attention is naturally drawn to the "eyes" of a home, the windows, skylights and glass doors.

These very important structural features, when expertly planned and designed, add personality and distinction to your interior while complementing the exterior architectural style of your home.

After lumber, windows are the most expensive part of a home. Take the time to investigate the various features and qualities of windows, skylights and glass doors. Visit a specialty store offering top of the line products and service and take advantage of their awareness of current products as well as their accumulated knowledge.

Visit a showroom with your designer, builder or architect. Because of the rapidly changing requirements of local building codes, it's difficult for them to keep current on what can be installed in your municipality. In addition, the dizzying pace of energy efficiency improvements over the past five years can easily outrun the knowledge of everyone but the window specialist. Interior designers can help you understand proper placement and scale in relation to furnishings and room use.

As you define your needs ask questions about alternatives or options, such as energy efficiency, ease of maintenance, appropriate styles to suit the exterior architecture, and interior.

Top quality windows offer high energy efficiency, the best woodwork and hardware, and comprehensive service and guarantees (which should not be pro-rated). Good service agreements cover everything, including the locks.

Every home of distinction deserves an entry that exudes a warm welcome and a strong sense of homecoming. When we think of "coming home," we envision an entry door first, the strong, welcoming look of it, a first impression of the home behind it. To get the best quality door, contact a door or millwork specialist with a reputation for delivering top quality products. They can educate you on functionality, and wood and size choices and availability, as well as appropriate style. Doors are also made of steel or fiberglass, but wood offers the most flexibility for custom design.

Since doors are a permanent part of your architecture, carefully shop for the design that best reflects the special character of your home. Allow two to three weeks for delivery of a simple door and eight to 12 weeks if you're choosing a fancy front door. Doors are installed during the same phase as windows, before insulation and drywall.

FABULOUS HARDWARE ADDS DESIGN FLAIR

Door and cabinet hardware, towel bars and accessories add style and substance to interiors. Little things truly do make the difference - by paying attention to the selection of top quality hardware in long-lasting, great-looking finishes, you help define your signature style and commitment to quality in a custom home. There are hundreds of possibilities, so when you visit a specialty showroom, ask the sales staff for their guidance. They can direct you towards the products that will complement your established design style and help you stay within the limits of your budget. When a rim lock for the front door can easily cost $500, and knobs can be $10 each, the advice of a knowledgeable expert is priceless.

Most products are readily available in a short time frame, with the exception of door and cabinetry hardware. Allow eight weeks for your door hardware, and three to four weeks for cabinetry selections. Since accessory hardware is usually in stock, changing cabinet knobs, hooks and towel bars is a quick and fun way to get a new look. ■

LUXURY GLASS & MIRROR

• **Mirrored Exercise Room:** Floor to ceiling, wall to wall mirrors, on two or three walls. Allow at least a month, from initial measuring, to squaring off and balancing walls, to installation. Price for polished mirror starts around $9 per square foot. Cut-outs for vent outlets cost extra.

• **Custom Shower Doors:** Frameless, bent or curved shower doors are popular luxury upgrades. Made of clear or sandblasted heavy glass - 1/2" to 3/8" thick. $2,000 and up.

• **Stained Glass Room Divider:** Contemporary, clear on clear design, with a hint of color. Approximately 4' x 6', inset into a wall. $4,500.

• **Glass Dining Table:** Custom designed with bevel edge, 48" x 96" with two glass bases. $1,200.

Custom Cabinets

INTERIOR TRIM CREATIONS, INC...**(704) 821-1470**
Fax: (704) 821-1473
3603 Gribble Road, Stallings
See Ad on Page: 330, 331, 343
<u>Principal/Owner:</u> Antonio & Lin Valdez
<u>Website:</u> www.interiortrimcreations.com <u>e-mail:</u> itc2millwork@cs.com
<u>Additional Information:</u> Sixty plus employees dedicated to the highest quality
and service available in comprehensive manufacturing and installation of custom
interior millwork.

Interior Trim Creations

"Setting the Standard in Architectural Millwork"

3603 Gribble Road ~ Stallings, NC 28104
Phone: (704) 821-1470 ~ Fax: (704) 821-1473

Windows
& Doors

RALEIGH SPECIALTY PRODUCTS, INC. ....**(919) 783-5386**
8101 Brownleigh Dr., Raleigh   Fax: (919) 783-9003
See Ad on Page: 345
<u>Principal/Owner:</u> David Hillman

Custom
Metalworking

OLD WORLD IRON ....**(800) 569-3874**
1115 Dragon Street, Dallas   Fax: (972) 484-9758
See Ad on Page: 347
Principal/Owner: William Lee
Website: www.oldworldiron.com e-mail: teresa@oldworldiron.com
Additional Information: We fabricate stair balastrades, stair carriages, custom
entry systems, driveway gates, balcony rail systems & custom specialty items.

Only If You Want the Very Best...

The
Ashley
Group

1350 E. Touhy Avenue, Des Plaines, Illinois 60018
888.458.1750   Fax 847.390.2902

www.theashleygroup.com • www.homebook.com

Millwork

APPALACHIAN LUMBER COMPANY ....**(336) 973-7205**
5877 US HWY 421 N., Wilkesboro   Fax: (336) 973-5503
See Ad on Page: 332, 350, 351
Principal/Owner: William Church

THE HARDWOOD COMPANY ....**(800) 771-5006**
5877 West US Hwy 421 North, Wilkesboro   Fax: (336) 973-5503
See Ad on Page: 332, 350, 351
Principal/Owner: William B. Church, Jr.
Website: www.hardwoodco.com e-mail: hardwoodco@wilkes.net
Additional Information: Specializing in hardwood plank flooring, paneling, moulding, stair parts and is a premier distributor of Weather Shield.

LEGACY MILLWORK SPECIALTIES ....**(919) 361-0089**
105 Hwy 54 West, Suite 269, Durham   Fax: (919) 361-9341
See Ad on Page: 332, 350, 351
e-mail: LMS1199@mindspring.com

Legacy Millwork Specialties

105 Hwy. #54 West, Suite 269
Durham, NC 27713
Tel: (919) 361-0089
Fax: (919) 361-9341
E-mail: LMS1199@mindspring.com

"Unique Woods for Unique Homes"

Weather Shield
Windows & Doors

The Hardwood Company

1910 South Blvd.
Charlotte, NC 28203
Tel: (800) 222-3853
Fax: (704) 332-6222
E-mail: hardwoodco@wilkes.net

Weather Shield
Windows & Doors

Decorative
Glass & Mirrors

STAINED GLASS OVERLAY OF CHARLOTTE ....**(704) 845-1235**
9303 Monroe Road, Suite L, Charlotte   Fax: (704) 845-1372
See Ad on Page: 353
Principal/Owner: Patricia Conway
Website: www.staindedglassoverlay.com e-mail: jconway573@aol.com
Additional Information: Worlds largest decorative glass company plus mahogany doors & entrances.

ELEGANT PRIVACY

Simply Beautiful,
Custom Designed…
Windows,
Doors & Sidelights,
Mahogany Doors
& Entranceways,
Baths,
Transoms,
Cabinets,
and more . . .

Let us create
the perfect design
for you.

Fireplaces, Mantels, Moldings, & Columns

DE SANTANA STONE COMPANY ....**(800) 810-8838**
PO Box 15712, Asheville
Fax: (828) 687-1900
See Ad on Page: 356, 357
Principal/Owner: Jane Kennelly
e-mail: desantana@ioa.com
Additional Information: Established as this country's finest custom handcarved stone importer, De Santana excels at custom design in hand carved cantera and adoquin stone, Italian carved limestone, and Yucatan Limestone.

INNOVATIVE BUILDING PRODUCTS...**(704) 599-6606**
3010-D Hutchinson McDonald Rd., Charlotte
Fax (704) 599-6628
See Ad on Page: 358, 359
Principal/Owner: John Adams
Additional Information: Specializing in Isokern Fireplaces & Norco custom windows & doors

TODAY'S FIREPLACE ....**(704) 598-6090**
6601-A Northpark Blvd., Charlotte
Fax: (704) 598-4837
See Ad on Page: 355
Principal/Owner: David Nash
Website: www.todaysfireplace.com   e-mail: nashd@todaysfireplace.com

6601-A Northpark Blvd. • Charlotte, NC 28216
Phone: 704-598-6090 • E-mail: Nashd@todaysfireplace.com

ISOKERN®
Fireplaces and Chimney Systems

3010-D Hutchinson-McDonald
Office 704/599-6606

Fireplace and

INNOVATIVE BUILDING
PRODUCTS, INC.

Road • Charlotte, NC 28269
• Fax 704/599-6628

NORCO
WINDOWS & PATIO DOORS
BUILDING CONFIDENCE
PART OF THE JELD-WEN® FAMILY

Window Specialists

Location,
Location,
Location!

What better LOCATION for your
advertisement than the
NORTH CAROLINA HOME BOOK!

Just as our readers realize how important
location is when choosing a home, we realize
that it's just as important to you when
allocating your advertising dollars.
That's why we have successfully positioned the
NORTH CAROLINA HOME BOOK to reach
the high-end consumers you want as clients.

**Call 704-549-3687 to find out about our
unique marketing programs and
advertising opportunities.**

Published by
The Ashley Group
8420 University Executive
Suite 810
Charlotte, NC 28262
704.549.3687 fax: 704.549.3695
E-mail: ashleybooksales@cahners.com

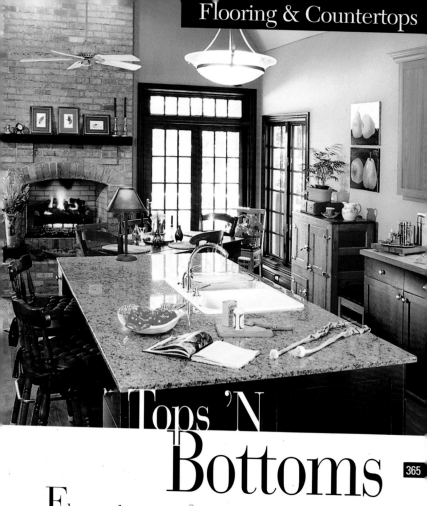

Tops 'N Bottoms

Floors and countertops, once thought of as merely utilitarian surfaces are now recognized as important design elements, admired as much for their beauty as for their strength. Because they occupy so much visual space they can set the tone for the entire house. From striking natural materials such as marble, granite, wood, tile, glass or metal, or one of the ever increasing array of luxurious man-made products, homeowners can select surfaces that are both suitable for the purpose at hand, while at the same time a stunning design statement in their home. By combining materials, talented artisans and craftsmen create enduring works of art that personalize the home and increase its value.

Imported from all corners of the world, floor coverings are on display and readily available in the finest area rug galleries. Beautifully crafted with rich, lustrous fibers and hues, they add drama and focus to any room.

In the following pages enjoy the work of talented craftsmen, who with unmatched skill and style, can take simple yet beautiful materials to create what could become the centerpiece of your home.

Photo courtesy of **Shaw/Davis Architects, P.A.**

FLOOR COVERINGS OF DISTINCTION...CARPETS & RUGS

From a room-sized French Aubusson rug to a dense wool carpet with inset borders, "soft" floor treatments are used in area homes to make a signature statement, or blend quietly into the background to let other art and furnishings grab the attention.

Selecting carpeting and rugs requires research, a dedicated search, and the guidance of a well established design plan. Because the floor covers the width and depth of any room, it's very important that your choices are made in concert with other design decisions–from furniture to art, from window treatments to lighting.

Your interior designer or a representative at any of the fine retail stores featured in the following pages is qualified to educate you as you make your selections.

Rug and carpet dealers who cater to a clientele that demands a high level of personal service (from advice to installation and maintenance) and top quality products, are themselves dedicated to only the best in terms of service and selection. Their accumulated knowledge will be a most important benefit as you select the right carpet for your home.

THE WORLD AT YOUR FEET

Today's profusion of various fibers, colors, patterns, textures, and weights make carpet selection exciting and challenging. Your search won't be overwhelming if you realize the requirements of your own home and work within those boundaries.

Begin where the carpet will eventually end up— that is, in your home. Consider how a carpet will function by answering questions like these:

• What is the traffic pattern? High traffic areas, like stairs and halls, require a stain resistant dense or low level loop carpet for top durability in a color or pattern that won't show wear. Your choices for a bedroom, where traffic is minimal, will include lighter colors in deeper plush or velvets.

• How will it fit with existing or developing decors? Do you need a neutral for an unobtrusive background, or an eye-catching tone-on-tone texture that's a work of art in itself?

• Will it flow nicely into adjoining rooms? Carpet or other flooring treatments in the surrounding rooms need to be considered.

• What needs, other than decorative, must the carpet fill? Do you need to keep a room warm, muffle sound, protect a natural wood floor?

• How is the room used? Do teenagers and toddlers carry snacks into the family room? Is a finished basement used for ping-pong as well as a home office?

ORIENTAL RUGS

The decision to invest in an Oriental rug should be made carefully. Buying a rug purely for its decorative beauty and buying for investment purposes require two different approaches. If you're buying for aesthetics, put beauty first and condition second. Certain colors and patterns are more significant than others; a reputable dealer can guide you. Check for quality by looking at these features:

• Regularity of knotting.
• Color clarity.
• Rug lies evenly on the floor.
• Back is free of damage or repair marks.

THE NUMBER ONE WAY TO DECIDE ON A RUG

Do you like the rug enough to decorate around it? There's your answer.

THE ARTISTRY OF RUGS

Nothing compares to the artful elegance of a carefully selected area rug placed on a hard surface. Through pattern, design, texture and color, rug designers create a work of art that is truly enduring. If you have hardwood, marble or natural stone floors, an area rug will only enhance their natural beauty. From Chinese silk, to colorful Pakistanis, to rare Caucasian antiques, the possibilities are as varied as the world is wide.

If you're creating a new interior, it's best to start with rug selection. First, it's harder to find the 'right' rug than it is to find the 'right' fabric or paint: there are simply fewer fine rugs than there are fabrics, patterns or colors. However, don't make a final commitment on a rug until you know it will work with the overall design. Second, rugs usually outlive other furnishings. Homeowners like to hang on to their rugs when they move, and keep them as family heirlooms.

In recent years, many rug clients have been enjoying a bounty of beautiful, well-made rugs from every major rug-producing country in the world. As competition for the global market intensifies, rugs of exceptionally high caliber are more readily available. Getting qualified advice is more important than ever.

Fine rug dealers, like those showcased in the following pages, have knowledgeable staff members who are dedicated to educating their clientele and helping them find a rug they'll love. Through careful consideration of your tastes, and the requirements of your home, these professionals will virtually walk you through the process. They'll encourage you to take your time, and to judge each rug on its own merits. They'll insist on you taking rugs home so you can experience them in your own light (and may also provide delivery). And their companies will offer cleaning and repair service, which may well be important to you some day.

ELEGANCE UNDERFOOT: HARDWOOD

A hardwood floor is part of the dream for many custom homeowners searching for a warm, welcoming environment. Highly polished planks or fine parquet, the beauty of wood has always been a definitive part of luxurious homes and as the design "warming trend" continues, a wood floor figures prominently in achieving this feeling.

With new product options that make maintenance even easier, wood floors continue to add value and distinction in upscale homes throughout the area and the suburbs. Plank, parquet, and strip wood come in a wide variety of materials, and scores of styles and tones. Consider what effect you're trying to achieve.

FOR SUCCESSFUL CARPET SHOPPING

1. Take along blueprints (or accurate measurements), fabric swatches, paint chips & photos.
2. Focus on installed, not retail price.
3. Take samples home to experience it in the light of the room.
4. Be aware of delivery times; most carpet is available within weeks; special orders or custom designs take much longer.
5. Shop together. It saves time in the decision-making process.

BUDGETING FOR WOOD FLOOR*

2 1/4" strip oak – $10/sq. ft.
Wider plank or parquet, glued & nailed – $15/sq. ft.
Fancy parquet, hand-finished plank or French patterns (Versailles, Brittany) – $30/sq. ft. and up.
* Estimates include finishing and installation; not sub-floor trim.

Plank wood complements a traditional interior, while parquet wood flooring offers a highly stylized look. Designs stenciled directly on to floorboards create an original Arts and Crafts feel.

The more exotic woods used for flooring, like Brazilian cherry wood, are often harvested from managed forests.

VINYL AND LAMINATES

Vinyl or laminated floor coverings are no longer considered candidates for immediate rehab.— as a matter of fact, they're among the most updated looks in flooring. Stylish laminates are made to convincingly simulate wood, ceramic tile and other natural flooring products, and are excellent choices for heavy traffic areas. They come in hundreds of colors and patterns, and offer great compatibility with countertop materials.

THE RENAISSANCE OF CERAMIC TILE

Ceramic tile has literally come out of the back rooms and into the spotlight with its color, beauty and unique stylistic potential. As sophisticated shoppers gain a better understanding of the nature and possibilities of tile, its use has increased dramatically. Homeowners who want added quality and value in their homes are searching out hand painted glazed tiles for the risers of a staircase, quirky rectangular tiles to frame a powder room mirror, and ceramic tiles that look exactly like stone for their sun porch or kitchen. From traditional to modern, imported to domestic, ceramic tile offers a world of possibilities.

It is the perfect solution for homeowners who want floor, walls, countertops or backsplashes made of top quality, durable and attractive materials. A glazed clay natural product, ceramic tile is flexible, easy to care for, and allows for a variety of design ideas. It is easily cleaned with water and doesn't require waxing or polishing. And, like other natural flooring and counter products, ceramic tile adds visible value to a luxury home.

SELECTING CERAMIC TILE

Not all tile works in all situations, so it's imperative that you get good advice and counsel when selecting ceramic tile for your home. Ceramic tile is wear-rated, and this standardized system will steer you in the right direction. Patronize specialists who can provide creative, quality-driven advice. Visit showrooms to get an idea of the many colors, shapes and sizes available for use on floors, walls and counters. You'll be in for a very pleasant surprise.

DON'T GET COLD FEET

Stone and tile floors are known for their chilly feel. Electrical products are available now to help warm the surfaces of natural products. Installed in the adhesive layer under the flooring, these warming units are available at the better suppliers and showrooms in North Carolina.

CERAMIC TILE AS STONE

With textured surfaces and color variations, ceramic tile can look strikingly like stone. You can get the tone on tone veining of marble, or the look of split stone, in assorted shapes, sizes and color.

If you're building or remodeling, your builder, architect, and/or interior designer can help you in your search and suggest creative ways to enliven your interior schemes. Individual hand-painted tiles can be interspersed in a solid color backsplash to add interest and individuality. Tiles can be included in a glass block partition, on a wallpapered wall, or in harmony with an area rug.

Grout, which can be difficult to keep clean, is now being addressed as a potential design element. By using a colored grout, the grout lines become a contrast design element—or can be colored to match the tile itself.

THE SOPHISTICATED LOOK OF NATURAL STONE

For a luxurious look that radiates strength and character, the world of natural stone offers dazzling possibilities. As custom buyers look for that "special something" to add to the beauty and value of their homes, they turn to the growing natural stone marketplace. A whole world of possibilities is now open to involved homeowners who contact the master craftsmen and suppliers who dedicate their careers to excellence in stone design, installation and refurbishing.

Marble and granite, which have always been options for homeowners are more popular than ever. With luxurious texture and color, marble is often the choice to add dramatic beauty to a grand entryway or a master bath upgrade. Granite continues to grow in popularity especially in luxury kitchens – there is no better material for countertops. It's also popular for a section of countertop dedicated to rolling pastry or dough. Rustic, weathered and unpolished, or highly polished and brilliant, granite brings elegance and rich visual texture that adds easily recognizable value to a home. Beyond marble and granite, the better suppliers of stone products also can introduce homeowners to slates, soapstone, limestone, English Kirkstone, sandstone, and travertine, which can be finished in a variety of individual ways.

CHOOSING STONE - A UNIQUE EXPERIENCE

Once a decision to use a natural stone is made, begin your search right away. By allowing plenty of time to discover the full realm of choices, you'll be able to choose a stone and finish that brings luster and value to your home, without the pressure of a deadline. If you order imported stone, it can take months for delivery. Be prepared to visit your supplier's warehouse to inspect the stone that

PRICING FOR NATURAL STONE

As with all flooring and countertop materials, get an installed, not a retail quote. Installation can drive the cost up significantly. Preparing a realistic quote may take days of research, due to the tremendous variety of factors that can influence price. As a general guideline, the installed starting price per square foot:
- Granite: $30
- Tumbled marble, limestone, slate: $20
- Engineered stone/ quartzite: $25
- Antique stone, with intricate installation: $75
- Granite slab countertop: $70

One Person's Project Estimate:

Reflooring
with
Red Oak

It's fun to imagine, but what might it actually cost to undertake a project described in this chapter? The example below describes a typical project and gives a general estimate of the costs involved.

Project Description

Replacement of the tile floor of a kitchen and breakfast area with red oak flooring, 200 - 250 sq. ft.

Removal and disposal of old flooring..$875

Installation of red oak boards, 2 inches wide.. $2,000*
(finishing fee included)

Toekick at base of cabinets $270

Inlaid vents that match the floor wood ($40 apiece).......................................$80

Threshold to different levels..$20

Furniture removed and replaced..$100

Cabinets wrapped during sanding $100

Total... $3,445

370

*Price is based on room with cabinets ($9/sq. ft.). If no cabinets exist, then the price is $8/sq. ft.

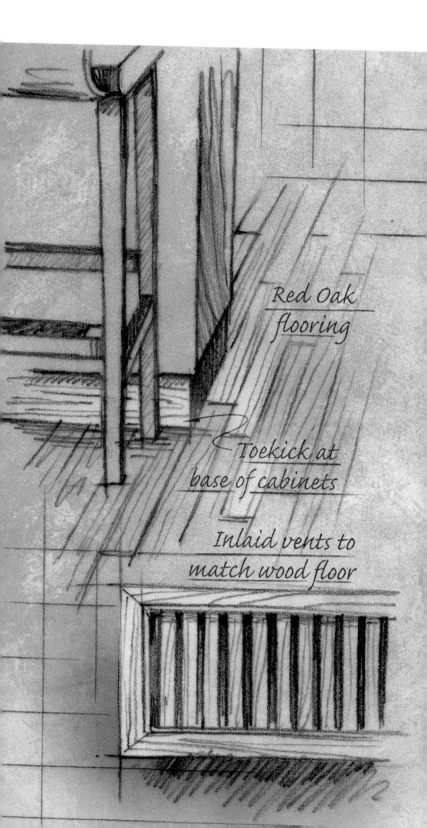

Red Oak
flooring

Toekick at
base of cabinets

Inlaid vents to
match wood floor

will be used in your home. Natural stone varies - piece to piece, box to box - a slab can vary in color from one end to the other. If you understand this degree of unpredictable irregularity is unavoidable, it will help you approach the selection in a realistic way.

STRONG AND ELEGANT COUNTERTOPS

The quest for quality and style does not stop until the countertops are selected. Today's countertop marketplace is brimming with manmade products that add high style without sacrificing strength and resiliency.

As the functions of kitchens become broader, the demand for aesthetics continues to increase dramatically. For lasting beauty with incredible design sensibilities, manmade solid surfaces are a very popular choice. The overwhelming number of possibilities and combinations in selecting countertops makes it vital to work with specialists who are quality-oriented. Countertops represent a significant investment in a custom home, and quality, performance and style must be the primary considerations in any decision. Established professionals, like those introduced in your Home Book, have a reputation for expert installation and service of the top quality products that define luxury.

MAKE COUNTERTOP CHOICES EARLY

Since decisions on cabinetry are often made far in advance, it's best to make a countertop choice concurrently.

Expect to spend at least two weeks visiting showrooms and acquainting yourself with design and materials. Take along paint chips, samples of cabinet and flooring materials, and any pictures of the look you're trying to achieve. Expect a solid surface custom counter order to take at least five weeks to arrive.

A WEALTH OF COUNTERTOP OPTIONS

You'll face a field of hundreds of colors and textures of solid surfacing, laminates, ceramic tile, natural stone, wood and stainless or enameled steel. Poured concrete counters also are finding their way into luxury kitchens in the area.

Laminate or color-through laminate offer hundreds of colors, patterns and textures, many of which convincingly mimic the look of solid surfacing or granite. Enjoying growing popularity in countertop application, are the natural stones, those staggeringly gorgeous slabs of granite, marble or

MAKE IT CONCRETE

This material is a versatile and indestructible choice, available in a variety of colors and textures. Sealed concrete can be made with creative borders, scored, sandblasted or stained. A strong, natural material, it can be made to look like other materials and natural stone.

SOLID SURFACING SHOWS UP ON TILES

Durable, non-porous solid surface materials are now being used to make decorative wall tiles. Check with your countertop supplier for information and ideas.

slate, which offer the timeless look of quality and luxury. Naturally quarried stone is extremely durable and brings a dramatic beauty and texture to the kitchen or bath. For endless color and pattern possibilities, ceramic tile is a highly durable option. Man made resin-based solid surfacing materials offer many of the same benefits as stone. These surfaces are fabricated for durability and beauty, and new choices offer a visual depth that is astounding to the eye. It can be bent, carved, or sculpted. Elaborate edges can be cut into a solid surface counter and sections can be carved out to accommodate other surface materials, such as stainless steel or marble. Best known for superior durability, solid surfaces stand up to scratches, heat and water.

FINDING THE BEST SOURCE FOR MATERIALS

If you're building or remodeling your home, your designer, builder or architect will help you develop some ideas and find a supplier for the material you choose. Reputable suppliers like those featured in the Home Book, are experienced in selecting the best products and providing expert installation. Go visit a showroom or office—their knowledge will be invaluable to you. The intricacies and idiosyncrasies of natural products, and the sheer volume of possibilities in fabricated surfaces, can be confounding on your own. ■

BEYOND TRADITIONAL

Solid surfacing is now being used to make custom faucets, decorative wall tiles, and lots of other creative touches for the home. Their rich colors (including granite), famed durability and versatility are perfect for bringing ideas to life. Check with your countertop supplier for information and ideas.

373

BE CREATIVE!

Mix and match countertop materials for optimum functionality and up-to-date style. Install a butcher block for chopping vegetables and slicing breads, a slab of marble for rolling pastry and bakery dough, granite on an island for overall elegance, and solid surfaces for beauty and durability around the sinks and cooktop areas.

Carpeting & Rugs

PERSIAN RUG HOUSE..**(704) 889-2454**
312 Main St., Pineville
See Ad on Page: 375
Principal/Owner: Reza Elyasi
Additional Information: The finest tradition has to offer. Monday-Saturday 10-5.

PERSIAN RUG HOUSE..**(800) 729-0349**
1437 E. Morehead St., Charlotte
See Ad on Page: 375
Principal/Owner: Reza Elyasi
Additional Information: The finest tradition has to offer. Tuesday-Saturday 10-5.

RUG CRAFTERS, INC...**(336) 294-1446**
5 Wendy Court, Greensboro   Fax: (336) 294-7034
See Ad on Page: 377
Principal/Owner: Phill Rosenbaum
Website: www.athomedesign-rugs.com   e-mail: phill@athomedesign-rugs.com

THE RUG ROOM BY DON LAMOR ....**(828) 324-1776**
2220 Hwy 70 East, Suite 459, Hickory   Fax: (828) 267-2423
See Ad on Page: 376
Principal/Owner: Steve McNeely, Phil Chamberlain, Richard Brantley
Website: www.therugroom.com e-mail: sales@donlamor.com
Additional Information: The most beautiful rugs are also the most affordable
at The Rug Room.

374

All Types of Rugs from Around the World

Don Lamor, INC.
2220 HWY. 70 S.E.
HICKORY, NC 28602
FOURTH FLOOR -
HICKORY FURNITURE MART
(828) 324-1776
(828) 324-9202
FAX (828) 324-1676
www.therugroom.com
Email: sales@don lamor.com

As more homeowners opt for a casual, yet elegant ambiance, rugs continue to grow in popularity

RUG CRAFTERS, INC.

Custom Rug Makers

5 Wendy Court
Greensboro, NC 27409

888-294-1446 Ph
336-296-7036 Fax

Ceramic Tile

LAUFEN CERAMIC TILE...**(704) 527-1355**
100 Clanton Rd., Charlotte   Fax: (704) 527-3577
See Ad on Page: 380
M.R. TILE & MARBLE, INC..**(704) 400-3773**
1816 Wexford Meadows Lane Apt. , Charlotte   Fax: (704) 717-9187
See Ad on Page: 379
Principal/Owner: Michael V. Rice
Website: e-mail: Tile@ctc.net
Additional Information: A member of H.B.A.C. (Home Builders Association
of Charlotte) specializing in natural stone & ceramic.
TILE COLLECTION INC. ....**(704) 541-8453**
11200 Carolina Place Parkway, Pineville   Fax: (704) 543-6649
See Ad on Page: 384
Principal/Owner: Matthew, Mark and Elaine Creasser
Website: www.tilecollection.com
Additional Information: Full service design, installation and fabrication. Voted
Charlotte's Best in Showroom and Installation. Family owned and operated.
WAGSTAFF TILE ....**(336) 292-4993**
3720-C Alliance Dr., Greensboro   Fax: (336) 292-6671
See Ad on Page: 381
Principal/Owner: Valerie Jeglinski
Website: www.wagstaff-tile.com e-mail: info@wagstaff-tile.com
Additional Information: Specialize in ceramic, porcelain, and stone. Decorative
Bath and Backsplash. Flooring-extensive collection. Designers on staff– many
vignettes to show ideas.
WALKER ZANGER...**(877) 611-0190**
11435 Granite St, Suite M, Charlotte   Fax: (704) 583-7000
See Ad on Page: 382, 383
Additional Information: Create your own unique vision in tile & stone with Walker
Zanger's luxurious collection of Handmade Ceramic Tile, Terra Cotta, Stone Tile &
Slabs, Mosiacs and Glass. 110-page Ceramic Tile catalog $16.00. 110-page Stone
catalog $16.00.

378

M.R Tile & Marble Inc
Specializing In Natural Stones & Ceramics

office: 704-717-9187
cell: 704-400-3773
email:tile@crc.net

" New designs with old values
A Member of H.B.A.C.
(home builders association of Charlotte)

Laufen Ceramic Tile

100 CLANTON RD. • CHARLOTTE, NC 28217

PHONE 704.527.1355 • FAX 704.527.3577

Wagstaff Tile

Elements of Nature & Design
Greensboro, NC
336-292-4993
www.wagstaff-tile.com

Lasting

Impressions.

Ceramic Tile · Stone Tile & Slabs · Mosaics · Terra Cotta · Glass Tile

Flooring

ALLIED FLOORING PRODUCTS ....**(704) 522-0597**
3013 Bank St., Charlotte　　　　　　　　　　　　　　Fax: (704) 522-0598
See Ad on Page: 386, 387
Principal/Owner: Joel Martin
Website: www.alliedflooringproducts.com
Additional Information: Specializing in new installation & renovation of a wide variety
of quality hardwood flooring products.

Distinctive Hardwood Floors are Our Specialty.

Allied Flooring Products specializes in all aspects of hardwood flooring, from refinishing and repair to new installation.

Our hardwood floors have been featured in Home-A-Rama

Choose from a variety of hardwoods such as Brazilian Cherry, Red Oak, Black Walnut and Hard Maple. Our professionals even provide custom borders and accents to enhance your flooring.

For a free in home consultation, please call Allied Flooring Products at **704.522.0597.**

ALLIED FLOORING PRODUCTS

3013 Bank St. • Charlotte

Marble &
Granite

FORUM..**(704) 523-1255**
4111 South Blvd., Charlotte
Fax: (704) 523-3990
See Ad on Page: 364
<u>Principal/Owner:</u> Rick and Deborah Webb
<u>Additional Information:</u> Forum- truly a gathering of the world's finest materials.
Your source for the most unique and enduring products for your home.

GRANITE AND MARBLE BY MALAVE ....**(336) 273-0223**
150 Industrial Ave, Greensboro
Fax: (336) 273-0699
See Ad on Page: 362, 363, 390
<u>Principal/Owner:</u> Len Malave
<u>e-mail:</u> malave1gso@aol.com

MARBLE & GRANITECH, INC....**(704) 525-2345**
414 Foster Ave., Charlotte
Fax: (704) 525-2395
See Ad on Page: 288, 289, 389
<u>Principal/Owner:</u> Jeff Heldreth
<u>Website:</u> www.mgimarblegranite.com

In the World of Stone, we Believe in the Human Touch

Finally...
North Carolina's Own
Home & Design
Sourcebook

The **North Carolina Home Book** is your final destination when searching for home remodeling, building and decorating resources. This comprehensive, hands-on sourcebook to building, remodeling, decorating, furnishing and landscaping a luxury home is required reading for the serious and discriminating homeowner. With more than 500 full-color, beautiful pages, the **North Carolina Home Book** is the most complete and well-organized reference to the home industry. This hard-cover volume covers all aspects of the process, includes listings of hundreds of industry professionals, and is accompanied by informative and valuable editorial discussing the most recent trends. Ordering your copy of the **North Carolina Home Book** now can ensure that you have the blueprints to your dream home, in your hand, today.

O R D E R   F O R M

Solid Surfaces

SILESTONE OF NORTH CAROLINA ....**(704) 238-1659**
2809 Gray Fox Road, Monroe   Fax: (704) 238-8910
See Ad on Page: 392
Principal/Owner: Betsy Smith & Mario Gonzalez

STRENGTH & ELEGANCE

Sensational grace and endurance combine to create a timeless tradition. We at Silestone offer you a surface that will stand the same test of time. We bring the elegance of natural stone with added strength and durability to your home.

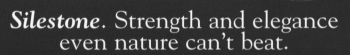

Silestone. Strength and elegance even nature can't beat.

Crafted from the finest quartz, Silestone is an engineered stone that is more durable than plastic solid surface or any natural material...including granite. Stain, heat and scratch resistant, Silestone is your low maintenance countertop for today's kitchen and bath.

With a luxurious array of colors, Silestone will compliment your kitchen, whether you are classically traditional or contemporarily modern.

THE LEADER IN QUARTZ SURFACING

Silestone of North Carolina
704.238.1659
www.silestoneusa.com

Stone, Slate
& Concrete

ARCHITECTURAL CONCEPT STONE ....**(803) 802-0686**
9072 Northfield Drive, Fort Mill   Fax: (803) 802-1765
See Ad on Page: 279, 394, 395
<u>Principal/Owner:</u> Kevin Sexton
<u>Website:</u> www.arcconceptstone.com
<u>Additional Information:</u> Custom architectural precast featuring decks, copings,
fireplaces, columns, window surrounds, sills, and anything you design.

EXTERIOR EXPRESSIONS...**(704) 708-5898**
1508 Industrial Dr, Matthew   Fax: (704) 708-5899
See Ad on Page: 232, 233, 396

INSTILE & LW CONTRACTORS ....**(704) 665-8880**
801 Pressley Rd., Suite 107-108, Charlotte   Fax: (704) 665-8182
See Ad on Page: 397
<u>Principal/Owner:</u> Lennart Wiktorin
<u>Additional Information:</u> Toll Free numbers: Instile 888-446-7845; LW Contractors
800-235-2882

393

ARCHITECTURAL CONCEPT STONE

9072 Northfield Dr. • Fort Mill, NC 29715
803.802.0686 • fax: 803.802.1765

INSTILE STONE & LW

Tile Roof

Cast-Stone

Travertine

Limestone Columns

Limestone Mouldings

Marble   Granite   Slabs   Tiles
888-446-7845

Finally...
North Carolina's Own
Home & Design
Sourcebook

The **North Carolina Home Book** is your final destination when searching for home remodeling, building and decorating resources. This comprehensive, hands-on sourcebook to building, remodeling, decorating, furnishing, and landscaping a luxury home is required reading for the serious and discriminating homeowner. With more than 500 full-color, beautiful pages, the **North Carolina Home Book** is the most complete and well-organized reference to the home industry. This hardcover volume covers all aspects of the process, includes listings of hundreds of industry professionals, and is accompanied by informative and valuable editorial discussing the most recent trends. Ordering your copy of the **North Carolina Home Book** now can ensure that you have the blueprints to your dream home, in your hand, today.

Order your copy now!

Published by
The Ashley Group
8420 University Executive
Suite 810
Charlotte, NC 28262
704.549.3687 fax: 704.549.3695
E-mail: ashleybooksales@cahners.com

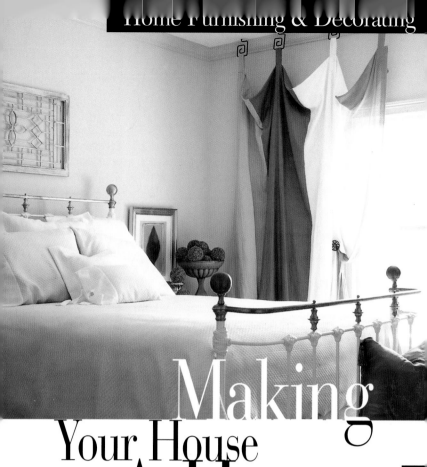

Making
Your House
A Home

A beautiful designed, meticulously planned house becomes a warm, welcoming home when the furnishings are finally put in place. Comfortably upholstered sofas and chairs in the family room, a unique faux-finished foyer, richly appointed windows in the dining room, all give a home its individual flair and peaceful comfort.

Today's homeowners, whether they're in their first or final home, have the elevated taste that comes from exposure to good design. They know what quality furniture looks and feels like and they want it in their homes.

In the home furnishing industry, choice is adundant, one item is more outrageously gorgeous than the next, and anything you can imagine can be yours. This freedom can be overwhelming, even intimidating, if you don't keep a sharp focus. By visiting the finest stores, specialty shops, and artisans, like those presented in the following pages, you'll find your quest for fine quality is already understood, and knowledgeable professionals are ready to guide you. Enjoy.

Photo courtesy of **Dina Lowery's Studio of Design**
Photo by **Pat Shanklin**

TAKE TIME TO CHOOSE FURNITURE

You'll be living with your choices for many years to come, so take your time. Try to define why you like what you like. Look through shelter magazines, visit decorator homes and furniture showrooms. When you see a piece or arrangement you like, try to analyze what you like about it. Is it the color, the style of the piece, the texture of the fabric? Recognizing common elements you are drawn to will help you hone and refine your personal style.

As you start out, be sure to ruthlessly assess your current interior. Clear out pieces that need to be replaced or no longer work with your lifestyle, even if you have no clear idea of what you'll be replacing them with. Sometimes empty space makes visualizing something new much easier.

When furnishing a new room, consider creating a focus by concentrating on an architectural element, or selecting one important piece, like a Chinese Chippendale-style daybed or an original Arts & Crafts spindle table. Or, make your focus a special piece you already own.

To make the most of your time when visiting showrooms, take along your blueprint or a detailed drawing with measurements, door and window placements, and special architectural features. If your spouse or anyone else will be involved in the final decision, try to shop together to eliminate return trips. The majority of stores can deliver most furniture within eight weeks, but special custom pieces may take up to 16 weeks.

Be open-minded and accept direction. Rely on your interior designer, or a qualified store designer, to help direct your search and keep you within the scale of your floor plan. Salespeople at top stores can help you find exactly what you're seeking, and, if you ask them, guide you away from inappropriate decisions toward more suitable alternatives. His or her firsthand knowledge of pricing, products and features is invaluable when it comes to finding the best quality for your money.

CONSIDERING CUSTOM FURNITURE

The ultimate in expression of personal style, a piece of custom designed furniture is akin to functional art for your home. A custom furniture designer can create virtually any piece you need to fill a special space in your home and satisfy your desire for owning a unique, one-of-a-kind.

Some of the most-talented, best known designers working in this area today are listed in the following pages of the Home Book. You can contact

MODERN IDEAS

With an evolutionary array of styles, contemporary furnishings add excitement, elegance and personality to a home. From Bauhaus, Retro, and Deco, to pure modern, these artful furnishings satisfy the desire for unique, individual expression.

KEEP IT ALIVE!

Regardless of your budget, you needn't sacrifice quality or style. Set your priorities and let your home take on a dynamic, ever-changing feel as you add or replace furnishings over a period of time.

them directly, or through your interior designer. At an initial meeting you'll see examples of the designer's work and answer questions like:

• What kind of piece do you want? Freestanding entertainment system, dining table, armoire?

• What functions must it serve? It is a piece of art, but the furniture still must function in ways that make it practical and usable. Explain your needs clearly.

• Do you have favorite woods, materials or colors? As with ordering custom woodwork, the possibilities are almost unlimited. Different woods can be painted or finished differently for all kinds of looks. It's best to have some ideas in mind.

• Are you open to new ideas and approaches? If you'd like the designer to suggest new ways of reaching your goal, let him or her know.

Seek out a furniture designer whose portfolio excites you, who you can communicate with, and you trust to deliver your project in a top quality, professional manner. Ask for a couple of design options for your piece. Make sure you and the designer are in agreement regarding finishes, materials, stain or paint samples you want to see, and a completion date. Most charge a 50 percent deposit at the beginning with the balance due upon completion. If you decide not to go ahead with construction of a piece, expect to be billed a designer's fee. A commissioned piece of furniture requires a reasonable amount of time to get from start to finish. If you want an entertainment system for Super Bowl Sunday, make your final design decisions when you take down the Halloween decorations. Keep in mind that the process cannot be rushed.

THREE IS THE MAGIC NUMBER

In accessorizing a home, thinking in "threes" is a good rule of thumb: Three candlesticks with candles of three different heights. Three colors of pottery grouped together, one less vibrant to highlight the others. Three patterns in a room.

405

SPOTLIGHT ON LIGHTING

Lighting can be the focal point of a room, or it can be so subtle that it's almost invisible. The trick is knowing what you want to accomplish. Indeed, when we remember a place as cozy, elegant, or dramatic, or cold and uncomfortable, we're feeling the emotional power of illumination.

The industry is filled with options and combinations, from fixtures and bulbs to dimmers and integrated systems. Top lighting retailers in the area employ in-house design consultants to guide you, or you can employ a residential lighting designer.

To deliver a superior lighting scheme, a designer must know:

One Person's Project Estimate:

Custom Designing a Cherry Wood Table

It's fun to imagine, but what might it actually cost to undertake a project described in this chapter? The example below describes a typical project and gives a general estimate of the costs involved.

Project Description

Custom design and construction of a 48" x 96" dining room table.

A couple moving to a new home in another region had trees from their old home site harvested, sawed into lumber, dried, and built it into a Cherry table for their dining room.

Trees harvested (felled) ($30/hr x 2 hours).. $60

Trees sawn and dried.. $175

Design (included in the project cost)
Clients were first asked about their desires for the table, then books and catalog research was done for examples. Once a basic concept is formulated, a full-scale drawing is done. Generally, clients may or may not see it these drawings. In this case, the clients only saw rough sketches before it was delivered to them.

Labor Cost $5,000
Fine sanding, construction, varnishing

Special materials (included in cost)..$0
Varnish, etc.

*Delivery (local) $0

Total: $5,235

Cherry tree harvested from old home site

Custom made dining room table

LOFT LIGHTING

Lofts do have large windows, but they're usually on one wall. That presents a lighting challenge that is often met with new low-voltage systems. The transformer is hidden in a closet or soffit; decorative transformers are mounted on a wall. The halogen bulbs last thousands of hours — very important given the height of loft ceilings.

A BRIGHT IDEA

Buy a few clip-on lights with 50-watt bulbs and take them home with you to pinpoint your needs and favorite lighting looks. Experiment with them to create different effects. See if you like up–or downlights to highlight an architectural feature. Get an idea of how much light it takes to illuminate a room.

• What is your budget? One of the biggest mistakes custom home owners make is under budgeting for their lighting program.

• What are your needs? Lighting falls into three categories—general, task, and atmospheric. A study/work area, a cozy nook, and a kitchen each require different lighting.

• What feeling are you trying to create?

• What "givens" are you working with? Where are your windows or skylights? The use of artificial, indoor light depends to a great degree on the natural light coming in.

• What materials are on the floor and what colors are on the walls and ceiling? This affects how well your lighting will reflect, or "bounce."

• Where is your furniture placed, and how big are individual pieces? This is especially important when you're choosing a dining room chandelier.

• If you're replacing lighting, why are you replacing it? Know the wattage, for instance, if a current light source is no longer bright enough.

• Are there energy/environmental concerns? Lighting consumes 12 to 15 percent of the electricity used in the home. An expert can develop a plan that maximizes energy efficiency.

• Who lives in the house? Will footballs and frisbees be flying through the kitchen? Take a pass on the hanging fixture and choose recessed lighting instead.

WINDOW DRESSING

The well-appointed room includes window treatments in keeping with the style of the home and furnishings. Yet it's also important to consider how your window treatments will need to function in your setting. Will they be required to control light, or provide privacy as well? Some windows in your home may need just a top treatment as a finishing touch, while a soaring window wall might require sun-blocking draperies or blinds to minimize heat build-up or ultraviolet damage.

How window treatments will be installed is another design question to consider–inside or outside the window frame, from the top of the window to the sill or from ceiling to floor? Take these points into consideration when designing your window treatments:

• How much privacy do you require? If you love the look of light and airy sheers, remember they become transparent at night and you may need blinds or shades as well.

• Is light control necessary? This is usually a must for bedroom window treatments, as well as for windows with southern or western exposures.

• Do you want to take advantage of a beautiful view of the landscape or hide an unsightly view of the building next door?

• Are there any structural elements such as built-in cabinets, outlets or vents near the window to consider?

• Are your windows a focal point of the room or the background that puts the finishing touch on your room design?

• What role will the choice of fabric play? The fabric can unify the whole, standout as the focus, or add another note to the rhythm of the room.

PAINTING OUTSIDE THE FRAMES

Through their travels, reading and exposure to art and design, sophisticated homeowners are aware of the beauty that can be added to their homes with specialty decorative painting. They see perfect canvases for unique works of art in walls, furniture and fabrics. The demand for beautiful art applied directly to walls, stairs or furniture has created a renaissance in decorative painting. Faux finishes, trompe l'oeil and murals have joined the traditional finishes of paint, wallpaper and stain for consideration in outstanding residential interiors.

Specialty painters of the highest caliber, such as those on these pages, can help you fine-tune your idea, or develop a concept from scratch. At your initial meeting, discuss your ideas, whether they're crystal clear or barely there. Don't be apprehensive if you don't have a clear idea. Artists are by profession visually creative, and by asking questions and sharing ideas, you can develop a concept together. If all decision-makers can attend these meetings, the process will move along more quickly.

Ask to see samples of his or her other work, and if possible, visit homes or buildings where the work has been done. Ask for, and call, references. Find out if the work was completed on time and on budget. Based on your initial conversations, a painter can give you a rough estimate based on the size of the room and the finish you've discussed. You can expect the artist to get back to you with sample drawings, showing color and technique, usually within a week.

A deposit is generally required, with balance due at completion. Discuss payment plans in the initial meeting. Surface preparation, such as stripping and patching, is not usually done by the specialty

THE GLOBAL MARKET-PLACE

There are so many exciting lighting designs available from all over the world, a lighting retailer can't possibly show you even half of them in the showroom. Allow yourself enough time to pour over the catalogs of beautiful chandeliers, luminaries (lamps) and other lighting fixtures available to you. A special order may take up to eight weeks, but it may net you the most beautiful piece of art in your room!

409

LIGHTING YOUR ENTERTAINMENT ROOM

One suggestion for properly lighting a 20-foot by 20-foot room to be used for watching television, listening to music and entertaining friends:
• General lighting provided by recessed fixtures
• A wall-mounted dimming package, with remote control
• A decorative ceiling fixture for more lighting when entertaining.

THE PRICE OF GETTING ORGANIZED

- An eight-foot closet, round steel chrome-planted rods, double and single hang, with a five-drawer unit: $800 to $1,000

- His and Hers walk-in closet, full length and double hang rods, two five-drawer units, foldable storage space, mirrored back wall, shoe rack: $1,000 to $4,000

- Conversion of a full-size bedroom into closet area with islands, custom designed cabinets with full extension drawers and decorative hardware, mirrors, jewelry drawers, and many other luxury appointments: $15,000

- Customized desk area, with file drawers, computer stand and slide shelves for printer, keyboard and mouse pad, high pressure surface on melamine with shelves above desk: $1,000

- Average garage remodel, with open and closed storage, sports racks for bikes and fishing poles, a small workbench, and a 4-by-8-foot pegboard, installed horizontally: $2,500

410

painter. Ask for recommendations of professionals to do this work if you don't have a painter you already use.

Before painting is begun in your home, the artist should provide you with a custom sample large enough to provide a good visual sense of what the technique will look like in your home, with your fabric, woodwork and cabinetry.

"DECKED OUT" FOR OUTDOOR LIVING

As homeowners strive to expand comfortable living space into their yards, top quality outdoor furniture manufacturers respond with new and innovative styles. Before you shop for outdoor furniture, think about:

- What look do you like? The intricate patterns of wrought iron? The smooth and timeless beauty of silvery teak wood? The sleek design of sturdy aluminum?

- What pieces do you need? Furnishing larger decks and terraces requires careful planning.

- Will you store the furniture in the winter or will it stay outdoors under cover?

- Can you see the furniture from inside the house? Make sure the outdoor furnishings won't distract from the established inside or outside design.

THE SPECIAL QUALITY OF PIANOS

A new or professionally reconditioned piano makes an excellent contribution to the elegance and lifestyle of a growing number of area homes. Pianos add a dimension of personality that no ordinary piece of furniture can match. They are recognized for their beauty, visually and acoustically.

First time piano buyers may be astonished at the range of choices they have and the variables that will influence their eventual decision. Go to the showrooms that carry the best brand name pianos. Not only will you be offered superior quality instruments, but you'll also get the benefit of the sales staff's professional knowledge and experience. Questions that you need to answer will include:

- Who are the primary players of the instrument?

- What level of players are they (serious, beginners)?

- Who are their teachers?

- What is the size of the room the piano will be placed in?

- What are your preferences in wood color or leg shape?

• Are you interested in software packages that convert your instrument into a player piano?

Pianos represent a significant financial investment, one that will not depreciate, and may actually appreciate over time. If a new piano is out of your financial range, ask about the store's selection of reconditioned instruments that they've acquired through trades. The best stores recondition these pieces to a uniformly high standard of excellence and are good options for you to consider. These stores also hold occasional promotions, when special pricing will be in effect for a period of time.

THE HOME OFFICE COMES INTO ITS OWN

The home office is rapidly becoming a "must have" room for many homeowners. More businesses are being operated from home, and increasing numbers of companies are allowing, even encouraging, telecommuting. Spreading out on the dining room table or kitchen table is no longer an efficient option.

Because the home office often requires specific wiring and lighting, be sure your architect, designer and builder are involved in the planning process. If you're simply outfitting an existing room to be your home office, designers on staff at fine furniture stores can guide you. However, it's still most practical to get some architectural input for optimum comfort and functionality of the space.

Unless you're designing a home office that will be architecturally separated from the rest of your home (such as a 'loft' office over the garage) it's a challenge to effectively separate work and home. As you plan a home office, ask yourself these questions:

• How do I work best? Close to the action or tucked away where it's quiet?

• How much space do I need? More than one desk, space for computer equipment and other technology, or reference books and files? Space for seeing clients?

• How many phone lines will I need? Do I like a window view? Consider natural light as well as artificial light.

• How will I furnish the office? Will the space also serve as a library or guest room? ■

'FAUX' FINISH TROMPE L'OEIL?

Any painting technique replicating another look is called a 'faux' (fake) finish. There are many methods to achieve wonderful individual effects. Trompe l'oeil (fool the eye) is a mural painting that creates illusion through perspective. A wall becomes an arched entry to a garden.

BLACKLION ....**(704) 541-1148**
Fax: (704) 541-1355
10605 Park Rd., Charlotte
See Ad on Page: 400, 401, 414
<u>Principal/Owner:</u> Nita and Bob Emory
<u>Website:</u> www.blacklion.com <u>e-mail:</u> customservice@blacklion.com
<u>Additional Information:</u> Blacklion is a multi-merchant retail gift, home furnishings and design center.

BLACKLION ....**(704) 895-9539**
Fax: (704) 895-6622
20601 A Torrence Chapel Rd., Cornelius
See Ad on Page: 400, 401, 414
<u>Principal/Owner:</u> Nita and Bob Emory
<u>Website:</u> www.blacklion.com <u>e-mail:</u> customerservice@blacklion.com
<u>Additional Information:</u> Blacklion is a multi-merchant retail gift, home furnishings and design center.

BLACKLION ....**(704) 979-5466**
Fax: (704) 979-5454
Concord Mills Mall, 8261 Concord Rd., Concord
See Ad on Page: 400, 401, 414
<u>Principal/Owner:</u> Nita and Bob Emory
<u>Website:</u> www.blacklion.com <u>e-mail:</u> customerservice@blacklion.com
<u>Additional Information:</u> Blacklion is a multi-merchant retail gift, home furnishings and design center.

SCOTIA RIDGE TRADING CO. ....**(704) 987-5168**
26052 North Zion Street, Cornelius
See Ad on Page: 413
<u>Principal/Owner:</u> Ranger Girodano
<u>Website:</u> www.scotiaridgetrading.com <u>e-mail:</u> RangerGiordano@aol.com

SCOTIA RIDGE
T R A D I N G   C O M P A N Y

Worldwide Purveyors of Fine Furnishings & Rare Antiques

At **Scotia Ridge Trading Company** in Cornelius, NC, you will find fascinating furnishings and accessories from around the world. **Ranger Giordano**, founder and owner, converted a quaint 1940's movie theater into an eclectic dreamspace of collectables. He travels the world to select unusual antiques and furnishings made of solid, reclaimed teak, mahogany, bamboo, oak, sleeping wood, seagrass…etc. Dining tables, chairs, buffets, beds, and much more, fill his industrial-style store. Large, reversed hand-painted glass globes from inland China are unique pieces of art that will only be found at Scotia Ridge.

ROMAN ARM CHAIR

Chinese Sideboard 1860c. built of solid Yuma (Chinese elm wood) hand carved and adorned with unique metal pulls.

20052 North Zion Street
Cornelius, NC 28031
704 . 987 . 5168
scotiaridgetrading.com

SCOTIA RIDGE
TRADING COMPANY

I-77 North, Exit 28, Turn right on Catawba Ave., Hwy 115, turn left, go 50 feet, turn right and cross the RR Tracks

Come Prowl the Aisles

Gifts, Home Accents, Decorative Accessories, Furniture, Interior Design,
Children's Items, Garden Accents, Holiday Gifts, Art & Antiques

BLACKLION ®

CHARLOTTE	LAKE NORMAN	CONCORD MILLS
10605 Park Road	20601-A Torrence	8261 Concord Mills
704/541-1148	Chapel Road	Boulevard
	704/895-9539	704/979-5466

Lighting

THE LAMP PLACE, INC....**(704) 523-7463**
3108 South Blvd./3800 Monroe Rd., Charlotte   Fax: (704) 523-8634
See Ad on Page: 416
<u>Principal/Owner:</u> Thelma Houck & Sandy Humphrey
<u>Additional Information:</u> The largest selection of lamps & shades in the greater
Charlotte area, for the past 22 years.

THE LAMP PLACE

"Where Service Is A Tradition"

- Lamps
- Lamp Shades
- Expert Lamp Making
- Custom Shade Making
- UL Approved Lamp Repair
- Pictures, Mirrors & Accessories

If the professionals at The Lamp Place don't have the perfect lamp or shade for your needs, they can make it for you. The 21-year-old specialty shop creates about 50 percent of their lamps from a variety of unique vases, figurines, pots, beautiful decorator and antique pieces.

3108 South Blvd. Charlotte • 704-523-7463
3800 Monroe Rd. Charlotte • 704-334-8035
2210 E. Main St. Albemarle • 704-983-2235
www.thelampplace.com

Window Coverings
Fabrics & Upholstery

REIDS DECORATING, INC. ....**(704) 541-0197**
8040 Providence Road, Suite 400, Charlotte   Fax: (704) 541-0198
See Ad on Page: 418
<u>Principal/Owner:</u> Lynne W. Steele
<u>Website:</u> www.reidsdecorating.com
<u>Additional Information:</u> Reid's in an unusual shop; open retail with totally custom products, with everything for the home or office.

Specialty Painters
& Wall Finishes

ED COUNCIL STUDIOS ....**(704) 358-8120**
814 Ideal Way, Charlotte
See Ad on Page: 421
Principal/Owner: Ed Council
e-mail: edcouncil@yahoo.com
Additional Information: Offering museum quality murals, tromp l'oeil, faux finishing
and Venetian plaster. Creating beautiful custom environments to taste for distinctive
residential & commercial clients.

PAINTED FINISHES ....**(704) 332-5332**
304 Meacham St., Charlotte   Fax: (704) 332-5335
See Ad on Page: 420
Principal/Owner: Daphne Dwyer

419

Painted
Finishes

304 Meacham Street
Charlotte, NC 28203
704.332.5332
704.332.5335 Fax

Specializing in:

- **Murals**

- **Trompe lóeil**

- **Portraits**

- **Faux & Custom Painting**

- **Commissioned Fine Art**

Ed Council Studios

704•358•8120
cell 704•236•3146
edcouncil@yahoo.com

841 Ideal Way
Charlotte, NC
28203

Home Office,
Closet & Garage

CALIFORNIA CLOSETS ....**(704) 527-5505**
4324 Barringer Drive Suite 110, Charlotte   Fax: (704) 527-5520
208 South Miami Blvd., Durham, NC   **(919) 598-3100**
See Ad on Page: 423
<u>Principal/Owner:</u> Steve O'Brian
<u>Website:</u> www.californiaclosets.com

life, stuff, storage – The Bedroom Closet.

The home is the heart of life. An ever changing story of ourselves, our family, our friends. A welcome retreat where we protect, nurture and sustain all that is needed and loved.

Let California Closets share 25 years experience with you to create the finest custom storage solutions for all the areas of your home. Live the way you dream. Call today for a complimentary consultation in your home.

704.527.5505 • www.calclosets.com
4324 Barringer Drive, Suite 110
Charlotte, NC 28217

CALIFORNIA CLOSETS®

Recreation &
Entertainment

NOSTALGIC SPORTS AND GAMES ....**(704) 540-8330**
8140 Providence Road, Suite 600, Charlotte   Fax: (704) 540-9622
See Ad on Page: 425
Principal/Owner: Debra & Jack Aufrance
Website: www.nostalgicsportsandgames.com   e-mail: nostalgicsports@aol.com
Additional Information: Nostalgic Sports and Games specializes in unique and
upscale furniture, décor, and gift items for home recreation, offices and businesses.

New in the

THE LAMP PLACE, INC.
Rabbit Lamp:
A Lamp Place design original, this porcelain lamp has French Country appeal, yet the neutral colors blend with any décor. It stands 30 in. high and features a silk shade, held in place by a whimsical rabbit finial styled with the look of ivory.

Photo by **Bill Gleasner**

ALLIED FLOORING PRODUCTS
Hardwood Flooring:
Knotty white oak and Brazilian cherry plank are two new, popular types of hardwood flooring. Five-inch wide knotty white oak flooring provides a rugged, distressed appearance with closed knots and other natural hardwood characteristics. Select grade Brazilian cherry plank offers unmatched hardness and durability, along with natural furniture-grade beauty, making it a favorite among designers. Both woods are available in a variety of stains to accent any room in the home.

BLACKLION

Dried Florals and Arrangements:

The natural look of dried florals and arrangements has become more popular for those looking to fill their homes with elements of texture and beauty. The use of branches, feathers, leaves and cones has become an essential part of many of the dried arrangements seen in homes today. Available arrangements can include a simple container of dried roses, branches and greenery, which add a stunning and elegant look to any home.

427

Accessories

INTERIORS MARKETPLACE..(704) 376-0575
2000 South Blvd., Suite 200, Charlotte
See Ad on Page: 402

know about so many different objects, time periods, and design, that it truly does take a lifetime to develop an expertise. The professionals at these establishments are first and foremost interested in finding you an antique that will impress and delight not only today, but also in the future. They usually prefer to have you invest in one or two good pieces, rather than in a handful of items that won't bring you as much pleasure in the long run.

VISITING ART GALLERIES

More than anything else, choosing to make beautiful, distinctive art objects a part of your home brings the joy of living with beautiful things into the daily life of yourself, your family and your guests.

The most important rule to know as you begin or continue to add art to your home is that there truly are no "rights or wrongs." Find what reaches you on an emotional level, and then begin to learn about it.

Use your eyes and react with your heart. Look at art magazines and books. There are many, beautiful periodicals, and just as many books published on artists and art genres. Visit the museums in town, and those in other cities as you travel. Go to the galleries. Visit many of them for the widest exposure to different possibilities. Let only your sense of beauty and aesthetics guide you at this point. Consider other constraints after you've identified the objects of your desire.

When you've found what really speaks to you on a personal level, start learning more about the artists who create art in that style, where it's available locally, and if it's within your budget. The more information you can take with you when you begin your shopping, the more help a gallery can be to you in your search.

EXPERT ADVICE

The most reputable art gallery owners and dealers have earned their reputation by establishing an expertise in their field, and serving their clients well.

Buying from these established, respected professionals offers many benefits. Their considerable knowledge of and exposure to art translates into opinions that mean a great deal. They've done considerable research and evaluation before any item gets placed in their gallery, and determined that it's a good quality item, both in terms of artistic merit and market value. You can also rest assured they will stand behind the authenticity of what they present in their galleries. Most offer free consultations, trade-back arrangements, and installation, and will help you with selling your art at some point in the future as your collection grows, you change residences, or your tastes change.

THE FALL SEASON

Fall signals the beginning of the art season. Galleries will open exhibits and the excitement is contagious. Ask to get on gallery mailing lists to stay informed of fall openings.

SEE THE SHOWS

North Carolina abounds with arts, antiques, and collectibles shows and festivals. These are great places to browse for and learn about thousands of items — from jewelry to pop culture collectibles. Local newspapers and magazines run announcements for these kinds of events, or ask your favorite gallery owner for information.

The Finesse of Fine Art

It's fun to imagine, but what might it actually cost to undertake a project described in this chapter? The example below describes a typical project and gives a general estimate of the costs involved.

Project Description

Analysis, research and procurement of six art pieces for a Mediterranean-style home.

Before the project began, the client established a budget based on the type of art desired (sculpture, drawings, paintings, tapestry), the quality of the art, scale (size of objects), and provenance (history and notoriety of the artist).

The art
A print for the hallway	$ 8,000
A classical bronze sculpture, 4 ft tall	$ 3,000
A still-life painting	$ 8,000
Two tapestries ($2,000 ea.)	$ 4,000
A Dufy painting	$32,000

Art total: **$55,000**

Additional expenses
Appraisal expenses	$750
Framing of pictures	$2,500
Installation and handling	$2,500
Insurance	$1,250/yr
Security system (motion detector)	$1,250
Consultation fees	
(Ten percent of art)	$5,500
(Hourly fee: $150/hr x 40 hrs)	$6,000

Includes analysis of art needs based on scale and style of house and artist preferences, research done on availability of art pieces and procurement of those pieces.

Additional expenses:.........................$19,750

Total:..................................... $74,750

Note: a project such as this one usually lasts 12 to 18 months

8' x 6'
Tapestry

Frame for
Dufy painting

VALUE JUDGMENTS

Buy for love, not money. This is the advice we heard time and again from the best art galleries. Not all art appreciates financially – often it fluctuates over the years according to the artist's career, consumer tastes, and the state of the overall economy. If you love what you own and have been advised well by a knowledgeable professional, you'll be happiest with your investment.

There is no upper limit on what you can spend on an art collection, or a single work of art, and there are no set standards for pricing. Gallery owners set prices according to their own standards, evaluations and experience, to represent a fair market value.

Set a working budget (possibly a per-piece budget) and let the gallery know at the outset what the guidelines are. This saves both you and the gallery time and energy. You'll be able to focus on items that are comfortably within the range of your budget. Buy the best quality possible in whatever category you like. You will appreciate the quality for years. Don't hesitate to do some comparison shopping. Although each art object is unique in itself, you may find another piece in the same style that you enjoy equally as well.

The best dealers understand budgets, and respect your desire to get good quality at a fair price. They are happy to work with enthusiastic clients who want to incorporate beautiful art into their lives. Ask if the dealer offers terms, if you're interested in making your purchases on a payment plan. Also inquire about return or exchange policies, consignment plans, consultations and trade-up policies.

Only deal with dealers who are helpful and present their art fairly. If you feel intimidated in a gallery, or feel the dealer isn't giving you the time and information you deserve to make intelligent choices, visit another gallery. Never buy art under pressure from a dealer, or to meet a deadline imposed by your interior design timetable.

GO TO AN AUCTION HOUSE

Attending an auction is an excellent way to learn about decorative arts, develop and add to a collection, and simply have a good time. Whether you attend as a buyer, seller, or observer, an auction is an experience that will enrich your understanding and enjoyment of the art and antiques world.

If you're a novice, it's important to choose a well-established auction house with a reputation for reliability. Try to be a patient observer and learn about the process as well as the value of items you may be interested in later on.

Buy a copy of the catalog and attend the viewing prior to the beginning of the auction itself. Each item, or "lot," that will be available for sale at the auction will be listed, and a professional estimate of selling

MATCHING ART TO ARCHITECTURE

If you're renovating an historic or old home of distinction, ask your favorite gallery owner or renovation specialist for guidance in choosing art that will fit your home.

MAKE AN APPOINTMENT

When you have identified a gallery or dealer you admire, call for an appointment to discuss your needs. Most professionals appreciate knowing you will be visiting at a specific time so they can have additional help on hand to attend to other customers.

price will be included. Professionals will be available during the viewing to answer questions and help you become familiar with the art objects as well as the process. Once bidding starts, it is done by "paddle," small numbered placards used to signal a bid, which are obtained before or during the auction.

CHOOSING AN AUCTION

Find out about interesting auctions from the proprietors of galleries you like, or ask to be added to the mailing list of a reputable auction house. With these sources of information, you'll be informed of events that will feature quality items of interest to you. Local newspapers and magazines also print upcoming auction dates and locations. The established auction houses that have earned a reputation for reliability and expertise generally have a single location where they hold their auctions. Sometimes an auction will be held at an estate site, or a seller's location.

Before attending the auction, spend some time researching the art or antique you're interested in bidding on, so you'll be informed about its value and can make an informed decision. Talk to people at the galleries. There also are books available that publish recent auction sales to help you get an idea of price and availability. Check your library or bookseller for publications like Gordon's Price Annual.

There seems to be an air of mystery and sophistication that surrounds auctions, but don't let that discourage you from discovering the auction experience. They are enjoyable and educational for anyone who is interested in obtaining or learning about art and antiques.

BE REALISTIC

For many of us, an auction might seem an opportunity to pick up an item at a bargain price. Realize that there may be bargains to be found, but in general, auctioned items are sold for a fair price. There may be a "reserve price," which is a private agreement between the seller and the auctioneer on the amount of a minimum bid.

If you educate yourself about the category you're interested in, you'll be at an advantage at an auction. It's equally important to research the market value of any lot you may be considering. Remember that there is an auctioneer's commission of 10 to 15 percent of the hammer price, to be paid in addition to the purchase price, as well as applicable sales taxes.

Auctions are essentially competitive in nature, with potential buyers bidding against one another. Wait to become an active participant until you've attended enough auctions to feel confident in your own knowledge, as well as in your understanding of the auction process. ■

TARNISH OR PATINA?

If your collection includes decorative metal objects like an engraved silver platter or brass handles on an antique chest, tarnish may become an issue. In some cases, the tarnish, caused by oxidation, can add subtle shadings and a beautiful patina to the piece. Before you polish, decide if the piece is more authentic with the tarnish. If so, relax and enjoy.

Finally...
North Carolina's Own
Home & Design
Sourcebook

The **North Carolina Home Book** is your final destination when searching for home remodeling, building and decorating resources. This comprehensive, hands-on sourcebook to building, remodeling, decorating, furnishing, and landscaping a luxury home is required reading for the serious and discriminating homeowner. With more than 500 full-color, beautiful pages, the **North Carolina Home Book** is the most complete and well-organized reference to the home industry. This hardcover volume covers all aspects of the process, includes listings of hundreds of industry professionals, and is accompanied by informative and valuable editorial discussing the most recent trends. Ordering your copy of the **North Carolina Home Book** now can ensure that you have the blueprints to your dream home, in your hand, today.

Order your copy now!

NORTH CAROLINA
HOME
BOOK

Published by
The Ashley Group
8420 University Executive
Suite 810
Charlotte, NC 28262
704.549.3687 fax: 704.549.3695
E-mail: ashleybooksales@cahners.com

Antiques

SARA H. BISSELL ANTIQUE FURNITURE AND DECORATIONS..(704) 366-4246
6401 Morrison Boulevard, Charlotte   Fax: (704) 366-4134
See Ad on Page: 442, 443
Principal/Owner: Mr. & Mrs. Smoky Bissell
HIGHSMITH ANTIQUES ....**(919) 829-5999**
106/107 Glenwood Ave., Raleigh   Fax: (919) 831-0434
See Ad on Page: 430, 431
Principal/Owner: Herb Highsmith

Architectural
Antiques

OLDE WORLD RECLAMATION ....**(704) 331-9133**
1432 West Morehead St., Charlotte   Fax: (704) 331-9447
See Ad on Page: 448, 449
Principal/Owner: Charles Kullman
Website: www.oldeworldreclamation.com e-mail: kreativwerks@excite.com
Additional Information: We specialize in locating unusual, original or reproduction
European garden, decorative and architectural pieces for architects, designers
and builders.

Only If You Want the Very Best...

The
Ashley
Group

1350 E. Touhy Avenue, Des Plaines, Illinois 60018
888.458.1750   Fax 847.390.2902

www.theashleygroup.com • www.homebook.com

Art Galleries

THE ARTFUL DODGER ....**(704) 847-7796**
    106 North Trade St., Matthews   Fax: (704) 847-7797
    See Ad on Page: 445
    <u>Principal/Owner:</u> Heidi C. Hodge
    <u>e-mail:</u> artful@att.net
DINA LOWERY'S STUDIO OF DESIGN ....**(704) 529-2680**
    3019 Selwyn Avenue, Charlotte   Fax: (704) 529-2686
    See Ad on Page: 190, 191, 432
    <u>Principal/Owner:</u> Dina Lowery
    <u>e-mail:</u> dinalowery@prodigy.net

- **Structured Cabling**

- **Home Cinema**

- **Multizone Audio**

- **Lighting Control**

- **Home Automation**

Design, Installation & Service

Tel : (803)-547-6921
Fax : (803)-802-2086
Toll Free : 1-888-807-7407

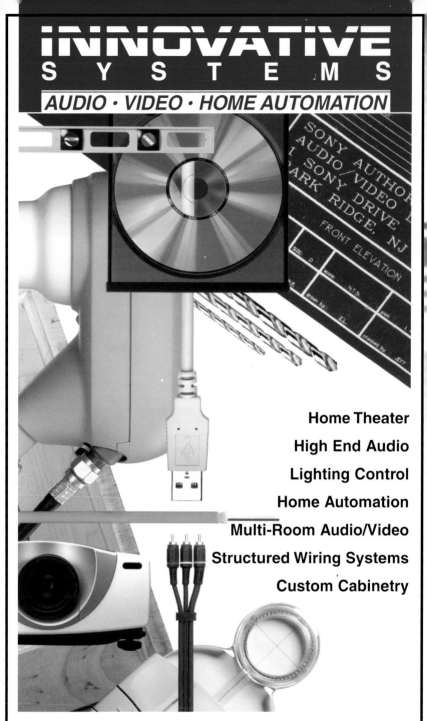

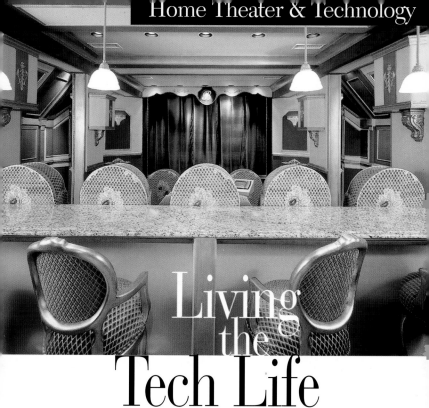

Living
the
Tech Life

Home technology just keeps getting better and better. Technology wizards continue to deliver bigger and better products less obtrusively, and more affordably, into our homes. What was once a rare home luxury has become a top priority item in new custom homes, and in home additions and renovations.

Sophisticated North Carolina homeowners have had their level of appreciation for quality in sight and sound elevated through the years of experience in concert halls, movie theaters and sports arenas. As they gravitate toward making the home the focus of their lifestyle, and strive to incorporate that high level of performance into their leisure time at home, home technology becomes a more desirable and practical investment. Systems are used for viewing commercial movies, home videos, live concerts and sport events, playing games, and accessing interactive technology. Media or entertainment rooms, custom-sized and designed to deliver concert hall sound and a big, sharp picture, are frequently specified in new construction and remodeling projects. Interest in upscale prefabricated home theaters, which are far more luxurious than some of today's movie theaters, continues to increase. "Hey kids, let's go to the movies!"

Photo courtesy of **David Simonini Custom Homes**

One Person's Project Estimate:

Your Personal Screening Room

It's fun to imagine, but what might it actually cost to undertake a project described in this chapter? The example below describes a typical project and gives a general estimate of the costs involved.

Project Description

Outfitting a room in the mid- to high-scale price range for a home theater

Initial consultation:.. $0

Labor:
$55/hour $3,500

50-inch television...$4,000

DVD player...$900

VHS..$200

Amplifier with surround-sound decoder...$10,000

Six speakers with subwoofer...$10,000

Satellite dish (high definition)..$1,000

Delivery/installation..$2,500

Seating: Eight leather module seats...$15,000

Infrared sensors (Crestrom) to control lighting,.....................................$10,000
motorized drapes, security system

Total $57,000

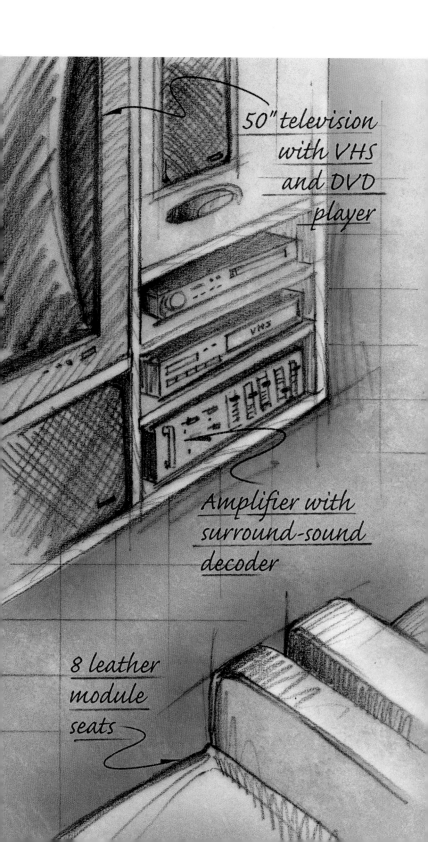

50" television with VHS and DVD player

Amplifier with surround-sound decoder

8 leather module seats

THE IMPORTANCE OF A HOME THEATER DESIGN SPECIALIST

Home theater is widely specified as a custom home feature today. The sophisticated homeowner with a well-developed eye (and ear) for quality demands the latest technology in a home entertainment system that will provide pleasure for many years. Because of the fluid marketplace, the vast possibilities of the future, and the complexity of the products, it's crucial to employ an established professional to design and install your home theater.

The experts presented on the following pages can advise you on the best system for your home. They can find an appropriate cabinet (or direct you to expect custom cabinet makers), expertly install your system, and teach you to use it. Their expertise will make the difference.

THE HOME THEATER DESIGN PROCESS

Tell your builder or remodeling specialist early if you want a home theater, especially if built-in speakers, a large screen or a ceiling-mounted video projection unit are part of the plan.

Inform the interior designer so proper design elements can be incorporated. Window treatments to block out light and help boost sound quality, furnishings or fabrics to hide or drape speakers, and comfortable seating to enhance the media experience should be considered. If you plan to control the window treatments by remote control, these decisions will have to be coordinated.

Visit one of the following showrooms. Be ready to answer these questions:

• What is your budget? There is no upper limit on what you can spend.

• Do you want a television tube or projection video system? A DVD player or hi-fi VCR? Built-in or free-standing speakers?

• Do you want Internet access?

• What style of cabinetry and lighting do you want? Do you want lighting or a built-in bar? How much storage is needed?

• What are the seating requirements? Seating should be at least seven feet from the screen.

• Do you want whole-house control capability so you can distribute and control the system from different rooms of the house?

• How will you incorporate the system with the rest of the room? Must the home theater room meet other needs?

• Do you want extra luxuries, like multiple screens, or a remote control system that allows you to dim the lights and close the draperies? Ask your salesperson for ideas.

458

• Will this room function in the future? As technology continues to change our lifestyle, plan for this room to grow and change as well. Ask your salesperson for advice.

Take your blueprints or pictures to a specialty store where an "experience room" is set up for firsthand testing of different components and knowledgeable consultants can answer your questions. Electronics is a complex subject, but a good consultant will educate, not mystify you.

An in-home consultation with the designer should take place early in the planning stages. You can discuss issues like speaker placement and location of wall control panels.

Before hiring a designer, make sure your service needs will be met in a timely and expert manner. Ask for the names of former and repeat clients for references.

Experienced audio-video or media consultants can astutely determine your needs. They can design and install an end product that is properly sized for your room, satisfies your desire for quality, and meets the terms of your budget. They respect cabinetry requirements and the decorating elements that must be addressed in the deliverance of a top quality home theater.

The media consultant should be willing to work with the architect, builder and interior designer to make sure your requirements will be met.

Home theaters are installed at the same time as the security and phone systems, before insulation and drywall. In new construction or remodeling, start making decisions at least two months before the drywall is hung. Allow four weeks for delivery and installation scheduling.

CREATING A HOME THEATER

For the best seat in the house, you'll need:

• A large screen television and/or projection video system (from 32-inch direct view up to 200-inches, depending on the size of the room). New, compact products are available now.

• A surround-sound receiver to direct sound to the appropriate speaker with proper channel separation.

• A surround-sound speaker system, with front, rear, and center channel speakers and a sub-woofer for powerful bass response.

• A hi-fi stereo VCR or DVD (digital video) player for ultimate audio and video quality.

• Appropriate cabinetry, properly vented.

• A comfortable environment, ideally a rectangular room with extra drywall to block out distractions. ■

PLAN AHEAD

Even if you aren't installing a home theater system right away, have a room designed to serve that purpose later. Get the wiring done and build the room an appropriate shape and size. Get the right antenna. Ask for double drywall for noise control.

THE FUTURE'S HERE

Smart homes, those with whole-house integrated control systems and computerized automation, even voice-activated automation, are a reality in the new century. Many professionals believe it will one day be as standard as central air conditioning. It will be commonplace for a system to start your morning coffee, crank up the furnace, close drapes during a downpour or send a fax.

BEST TIP:

Have phone lines pulled to every TV outlet in the house for Internet access and satellite reception.

Home Theater
Design

ABSOLUTE AUDIO ....**(704) 333-2424**
219 West Morehead St, Charlotte   Fax: (704) 333-2426
See Ad on Page: 463
<u>Principal/Owner:</u> Eric Paige
<u>Website:</u> www.charlottehifi.com   <u>e-mail:</u> info@charlottehifi.com
<u>Additional Information:</u> Perfecting the design and execution of fine audio, home entertainment and lighting control systems.

AUDIO VIDEO ONE ....**(336) 774-1088**
2451 W. Clemmonsville Rd., Winston-Salem   Fax: (336) 774-1225
See Ad on Page: 464
<u>Principal/Owner:</u> Ronald Schwartz Jr.
<u>Website:</u> www.avone.net   <u>e-mail:</u> ron@avone.net
<u>Additional Information:</u> Audio Video One has won international design award in both 1999 & 2001 for "Best Home Theater" by CEDIA. (www.cedia.org) for info.

CAROLINA AUDIO CONSULTANTS ....**(704) 588-0662**
218 Westinghouse Blvd., Suite 201, Charlotte   Fax: (704) 588-0656
See Ad on Page: 462
<u>Principal/Owner:</u> Will Dixson, Rusty Bennett
<u>e-mail:</u> wendixson@bellsouth.net, rustycac@bellsouth.net

INNOVATIVE SYSTEMS ....**(704) 847-7708**
9129 Monroe Rd, Suite 140, Charlotte   Fax: (704) 847-2474
See Ad on Page: 454, 466, 467
<u>Principal/Owner:</u> Dennis Tooley, Mike Simpson
<u>Website:</u> innovativesystems-av.com   <u>e-mail:</u> msimpson@innovativesystems-av.c
<u>Additional Information:</u> Voted Charlotte's Best Audio Video Custom Designer and Installer and Audio Video Store.

NTOUCH MEDIA ....**(704) 372-0991**
301 South McDowell Street, Charlotte   Fax: (704) 752-6027
See Ad on Page: 461
<u>Principal/Owner:</u> Chad Luke
<u>Website:</u> www.ntouchmedia.com   <u>e-mail:</u> Sales@Ntouchmedia.com

SMART HOME INNOVATIONS ....**(704) 567-5825**
6101 Idlewood Rd., Charlotte   Fax: (704) 567-5232
See Ad on Page: 465
<u>Principal/Owner:</u> Steven Bass
<u>Website:</u> www.electronichouse.net   <u>e-mail:</u> sales@intelligenthomes.net

You deserve to be *Ntouch*

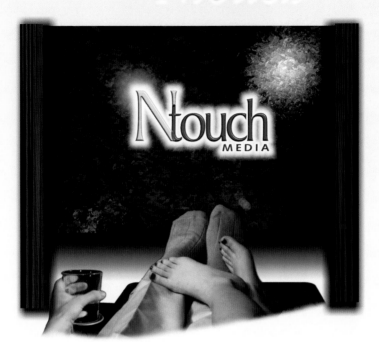

Ntouch Media presents
integrated entertainment and communications
solutions refined for the home. Experience the
difference of advanced technologies engineered
to create the perfect balance of performance, ease
of operation, reliability, and beauty. We are
committed to delivering unmatched service
and gratification for many years to come.

So sit back, relax, and enjoy life the way it should
be in your new dream home. Come visit us at our
website or schedule an appointment to see how
to get Ntouch with life at home.

www.ntouchmedia.com

301 South McDowell Street, Suite 706 Charlotte, North Carolina 28204

7 0 4 . 3 7 2 . 0 9 9 1

CAROLINA audio CONSULTANTS

- NEW EQUIPMENT SALES DESIGN & INSTALLATION
- CUSTOM HOME THEATRE
- HIGH DEFINITION TV
- MULTI-ROOM AUDIO & VIDEO
- STRUCTURED WIRING
- NEW CONSTRUCTION & EXISTING HOMES
- SHOWROOM BY APPOINTMENT

218 Westinghouse Blvd • Suite 201
Charlotte, North Carolina 28273
PH:(704) 588-0662 • Fax:(704) 588-0656

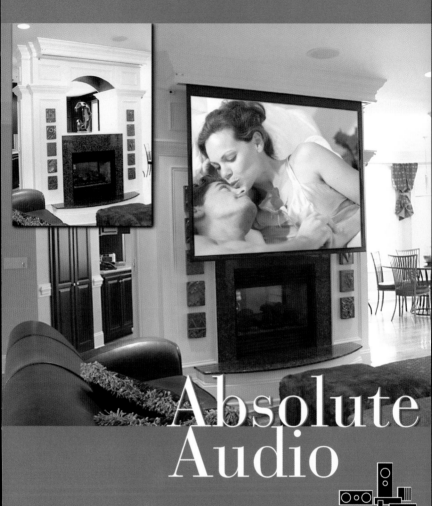

Practical Magic.

Custom Design • Home Theater
Multi-Room Audio/Video
Systems Integration

AUDIO VIDEO ONE

Home Entertainment Solutions

Custom Audio/Video
For the Future

INNOVATIVE
S Y S T E M S
AUDIO · VIDEO · HOME AUTOMATION

- **Home Theater**

- **High End Audio**

- **Lighting Control**

- **Home Automation**

- **Multi-Room Audio/Video**

- **Custom Entertainment Cabinetry**

- **Structured Wiring Systems**

Integrated
Home Systems

ADVANCED VISUAL ENVIRONMENTS..**(336) 852-5706**
4807-F Koger Blvd., Greensboro   Fax: (336) 855-5375
See Ad on Page: 470, 471
<u>Principal/Owner:</u> Richard Vanstory
<u>Website:</u> www.advancedvisualenvironments.net <u>e-mail:</u> kmikelonis@avenc.net
<u>Additional Information:</u> Specialists in design – Build services for music, video, communications and lighting control. Enhancing the fine home living experience.

INTEGRATED SYSTEMS CUSTOM AUDIO/
VIDEO SPECIALISTS ....**(803) 547-6924**
209 Williamson St., Fort Mill   Fax: (803) 802-2086
See Ad on Page: 452, 453, 469
<u>Principal/Owner:</u> George Lako Jr.
<u>Additional Information:</u> Specializing in design & installation of custom audio/video, lighting control and security.

${Integrated}$
Systems

Custom Audio & Video Specialists, Inc.

Philips

Elan

Parasound

Panasonic

Fujitsu

Member of
Para and Cedia

Tel : (803)-547-6921 • Toll Free(888) 807-7407

ADVANCEDVISUAL ENVIRONMENTS

ADVANCEDVISUAL ENVIRONMENTS

A Division of R.L. Vanstory Company

Home Theatre • Architechtural Electronics

4807 Koger Blvd. Suite F
Greensboro, NC 27407
Phone: (336) 852-5706
Fax: (336) 855-5375

330 Military Cutoff Suite A3
Wilmington, NC 28405
Phone: (910) 397-0018
Fax: (910) 397-2861

Group.com

THE HOME BOOK SERIES

The Home Book is a comprehensive hands-on design sourcebook to building, remodeling, decorating, furnishing and landscaping your luxury home. By logging onto www.theashleygroup.com, you can find out more information about our entire suite of Home Books in over 15 markets, (soon to be 23), as well as local design information in nine cities. It's also a great resource for investigating ideas and professionals in other cities where you might want to build or move into a vacation home.

THE DESIGN INDEX SERIES

The Design Index is the premier sourcebook designed to help the professional contact other professionals that they work with — every day, all day, all year long! Each spiral-bound directory contains thousands of listings and hundreds of beautiful visual pages. Each Design Index is city or region specific. Log onto www.theashleygroup.com and find out when the Design Index is coming to your city!

DESIGN BOOKS

Our design books represent the premier works of selected designers, luxury homebuilders and architects. these books showcase their most treasured works for that special person who enjoys luxury home and architecture stories. Log onto www.theashleygroup.com to find the design book that inspires you!

Only If You Want the Very Best...

The
Ashley
Group

Alphabetical Index

Professional Index

479

480

483

Professional Index

486

487

DESIGN

**The following design books represent the premier works
of selected designers, luxury homebuilders and architects.**

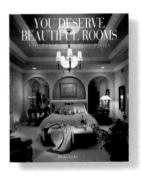

This book is divided into 10 chapters, starting with design guidelines in regards to color, personality and collections. In these chapters, interior designer Perla Lichi presents beautiful, four-color photographs of the design commissions she has undertaken for clients accompanied by informative editorial on the investment value of professional interior design.

YOU DESERVE BEAUTIFUL ROOMS
120 pages, 9.75" x 14"
Home Design, Architecture
1-58862-016-6 $39.95   Hardcover

Orren Pickell is renowned as one of the nation's finest builders of custom homes. In this collection of more than 80 beautiful four-color photos and drawings, Pickell shows off some of his finest creations to give homeowners unique ideas on building a new home or adding to an existing one.

LUXURY HOMES & LIFESTYLES
120 pages, 9.75" x 14"
Architecture, Home Design
0-9642057-4-2 $39.95   Hardcover

Designer Susan Fredman has spent 25 years creating interiors, which, in one way or another, have been inspired by nature. In this book, she takes readers through rooms which reflect elements of our surroundings as they are displayed throughout the year.

AT HOME WITH NATURE
136 pages, 11.25" x 11.25"
Home Design, Architecture
1-58862-043-3 $39.95   Hardcover

The Ashley Group is proud to present these specia

CALL TO ORDER

BOOKS

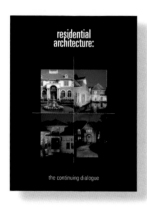

Michigan-based architect Dominick Tringali uses the skill and knowledge that has brought him over 20 industry awards to share strategies on building the ultimate dream house. By combining unique concepts with innovative techniques and materials, Dominick's portfolio displays an array of homes noted for their timeless appeal. This $45 million collection of elite, custom homes contains the residences of notable CEO's, lawyers, doctors and sports celebrities including Chuck O'Brien, Joe Dumars, Tom Wilson, Larry Wisne and Michael Andretti's estate in Pennsylvania.

**RESIDENTIAL
ARCHITECTURE:
THE CONTINUING DIALOGUE**
May 2002.
128 pages.
9" x 12"
Art & Architecture
1-58862-088-3
$39.95   Hardcover

Across the nation, homeowners often enlist the services of landscapers. Within this group lies an elite sector which specializes in breaking the mold on traditional landscaping. In this book, you will find truly groundbreaking approaches to the treatment of outdoor space.

**PORTFOLIO SERIES:
GARDEN DESIGN**
June 2002.
150 pages.
10" x 10"
Gardening,
Home Design
1-58862-087-5
$29.95   Hardcover

tles on luxury home style, design and architecture

888.458.1750

Notes

491

493

Notes

495

498